POETRY FROM CRESCENT
MOON

Walking In Cornwall
by Ursula Le Guin

Hymns To the Night
by Novalis

Hymns To the Night: In Translation
by Novalis

Flower Pollen: Selected Thoughts
by Novalis

Novalis: His Life, Thoughts and
Works
by Novalis

Edmund Spenser: *Heavenly Love:*
Selected Poems
selected and introduced by Teresa
Page

Edmund Spenser: *Amoretti*
edited by Teresa Page

The Visions of Petrarch and Bellay:
Early Sonnets
by Edmund Spenser

Robert Herrick: *Delight In*
Disorder: Selected Poems
edited and introduced by M.K.
Pace

Robert Herrick: *Hesperides*
edited and introduced by M.K.
Pace

Robert Herrick: *Upon Julia's*
Breasts: Love Poems
edited and introduced by M.K.
Pace

Sir Thomas Wyatt: *Love For Love:*
Selected Poems
selected and introduced by Louise
Cooper

John Donne: *Air and Angels:*
Selected Poems
selected and introduced by A.H.
Ninham

D.H. Lawrence: *Being Alive:*
Selected Poems
edited with an introduction by
Margaret Elvy

D.H. Lawrence: *Amores*
edited with an introduction by
Margaret Elvy

D.H. Lawrence: *Look! We Have*
Come Through!
edited with an introduction by
Margaret Elvy

D.H. Lawrence: *Love Poems and*
Others
edited with an introduction by
Margaret Elvy

D.H. Lawrence: *New Poems*
edited with an introduction by
Margaret Elvy

D.H. Lawrence: Symbolic
Landscapes
by Jane Foster

D.H. Lawrence: Infinite Sensual
Violence
by M.K. Pace

Percy Bysshe Shelley: *Paradise of*
Golden Lights: Selected Poems
selected and introduced by
Charlotte Greene

Thomas Hardy: *Her Haunting Ground: Selected Poems*
edited, with an introduction by
A.H. Ninham

Thomas Hardy: *Late Lyrics and Earlier*
edited, with an introduction by
A.H. Ninham

Thomas Hardy: *Moments of Vision*
edited, with an introduction by
A.H. Ninham

Thomas Hardy: *Poems of the Past and the Present*
edited, with an introduction by
A.H. Ninham

Thomas Hardy: *Satires of Circumstance*
edited, with an introduction by
A.H. Ninham

Thomas Hardy: *Time's Laughingstocks*
edited, with an introduction by
A.H. Ninham

Thomas Hardy: *Wessex Poems*
edited, with an introduction by
A.H. Ninham

Sexing Hardy: Thomas Hardy and Feminism
by Margaret Elvy

Emily Bronte: *Darkness and Glory: Selected Poems*
selected and introduced by
Miriam Chalk

John Keats: *Bright Star: Selected Poems*
edited with an introduction by
Miriam Chalk

John Keats: *Poems of 1820*
edited with an introduction by
Miriam Chalk

Henry Vaughan: *A Great Ring of Pure and Endless Light: Selected Poems*
selected and introduced by A.H. Ninham

The Crescent Moon Book of Love Poetry
edited by Louise Cooper

The Crescent Moon Book of Mystical Poetry in English
edited by Carol Appleby

The Crescent Moon Book of Nature Poetry From Langland to Lawrence
edited by Margaret Elvy

The Crescent Moon Book of Metaphysical Poetry
edited and introduced by
Charlotte Greene

The Crescent Moon Book of Elizabethan Love Poetry
edited and introduced by Carol Appleby

The Crescent Moon Book of Romantic Poetry
edited and introduced by L.M. Poole

Brigitte's Blue Heart
by Jeremy Reed

Claudia Schiffer's Red Shoes
by Jeremy Reed

By-Blows: Uncollected Poems
by D.J. Enright

Selected Poems
by William Shakespeare

Elizabethan Sonnet Cycles
by Daniel, Drayton, Sidney,
Spenser and Shakespeare

Elizabethan Sonnet Cycles (Volume
Two)
by Lodge, Griffin, Smith,
Constable and Fletcher

Three Metaphysical Poets
edited by A.H. Ninham

Three Romantic Poets
edited by Miriam Chalk

CHARLES BAUDELAIRE
HIS LIFE

CHARLES BAUDELAIRE
HIS LIFE

THÉOPHILE GAUTIER

TRANSLATED INTO ENGLISH, WITH SELECTIONS FROM HIS
POEMS, "LITTLE POEMS IN PROSE," AND LETTERS TO
SAINTE-BEUVE AND FLAUBERT AND AN ESSAY ON HIS
INFLUENCE
BY
GUY THORNE

(AUTHOR OF
"WHEN IT WAS DARK," "THE VINTAGE OF VICE" ETC.)

EDITED BY JEREMY MARK ROBINSON

WITH THE FRENCH TEXT

CRESCENT MOON

First published 1915. This edition © 2024.

Set in Book Antiqua 10 on 14pt.
Designed by Radiance Graphics.

British Library Cataloguing in Publication data

ISBN-13 9781861718037
ISBN-13 9781861719034

CRESCENT MOON PUBLISHING
P.O. Box 1312, Maidstone, Kent, ME14 5XU
Great Britain, www.crmoon.com

CONTENTS

NOTE ON THE TEXT

The text is from *Charles Baudelaire* by Théophile Gautier and Guy Thorne, published by Greening & Co., London, in 1915.

"Close to your hand lies a little
volume, bound in some Nile-green skin
that has been pounded with gilded
nenuphars, and smoothed with hard
ivory. It is the book that Gautier
loved, it is Baudelaire's masterpiece."

OSCAR WILDE ("Intentions").

Charles Baudelaire by Felix Nadar, 1855.

Charles Baudelaire by Gustave Courbet, 1849

THE LIFE AND INTIMATE MEMOIRS OF CHARLES BAUDELAIRE

BY THÉOPHILE GAUTIER

I

The first time that we met Baudelaire was towards the middle of
the year 1849, at the Hôtel Pimodan, where we occupied, near
Fernand Boissard, a strange apartment which communicated with
his by a private staircase hidden in the thickness of the wall, and
which was haunted by the spirits of beautiful women loved long
since by Lauzun. The superb Maryx was to be found there who,
in her youth, had posed for "La Mignon" of Scheffer, and later, for
"La Gloire distribuant des couronnes" of Paul Delaroche; and that
other beauty, then in all her splendour, from whom Clesinger
modelled "La Femme au serpent," that statue where grief
resembles a paroxysm of pleasure, and which throbs with an
intensity of life that the chisel has never before attained and
which can never be surpassed.

Charles Baudelaire was then an almost unknown genius,
preparing himself in the shadow for the light to come, with that
tenacity of purpose which, in him, doubled inspiration; but his
name was already becoming known amongst poets and artists,
who heard it with a quivering of expectation, the younger
generation almost venerating him. In the mysterious upper
chamber where the reputations of the future are in the making he
passed as the strongest. We had often heard him spoken of, but
none of his works were known to us.

His appearance was striking: he had closely shaved hair of a rich black, which fell over a forehead of extraordinary whiteness, giving his head the appearance of a Saracen helmet. His eyes, coloured like tobacco of Spain, had great depth and spirituality about them, and a certain penetration which was, perhaps, a little too insistent. As to the mouth, in which the teeth were white and perfect, it was seen under a slight and silky moustache which screened its contours. The mobile curves, voluptuous and ironical as the lips in a face painted by Leonardo da Vinci, the nose, fine and delicate, somewhat curved, with quivering nostrils, seemed ever to be scenting vague perfumes. A large dimple accentuated the chin, like the finishing touch of a sculptor's chisel on a statue; the cheeks, carefully shaved, with vermilion tints on the cheek-bones; the neck, of almost feminine elegance and whiteness, showed plainly, as the collar of his shirt was turned down with a Madras cravat.

His clothing consisted of a paletot of shining black cloth, nut-coloured trousers, white stockings, and patent leather shoes; the whole fastidiously correct, with a stamp of almost English simplicity, intentionally adopted to distinguish himself from the artistic folk with the soft felt hats, the velvet waistcoats, red jackets, and strong, dishevelled beards. Nothing was too new or elaborate about him. Charles Baudelaire indulged in a certain dandyism, but he would do anything to take from his things the "Sunday clothes" appearance so dear and important to the Philistine, but so disagreeable to the true gentleman.

Later, he shaved off his moustache, finding that it was the remains of an old picturesqueness which it was both childish and bourgeois to retain. Thus, relieved of all superfluous down, his head recalled that of Lawrence Sterne; a resemblance that was augmented by Baudelaire's habit of leaning his temple against his first finger, which is, as every one knows, the attitude of the English humorist in the portrait placed at the beginning of his books.

Such was the physical impression made on us after our first meeting with the future author of "The Flowers of Evil."

We find in the "Nouveaux Camées parisiens" of Théodore de Banville, one of the poet's best and most constant friends whose loss we deplore, a portrait of Baudelaire in his youth. We are permitted to transcribe the lines here, prose equal in perfection to the most beautiful verse. It portrays Baudelaire as he is very little known, and as he was only at that particular time.

"In a portrait painted by Émile Deroy, one of the rarest works of art by modern painters, we see Charles Baudelaire at twenty years of age, at a time when, rich, happy, well-loved, already becoming celebrated, he wrote his first verses which were applauded by Paris, the literary leader of the whole world! O rare example of a divine face, uniting all graces, power, and most irresistible seductiveness! The eyebrow well-marked and curved like a bow, the eyelid warm and softly coloured; the eye, large, black, deep and of unequalled fire, caressing and imperious, embraces, interrogates and reflects all that surrounds it; the nose, beautifully chiselled, slightly curved, makes us dream of the celebrated phrase of the poet:

'Mon âme voltige sur les parfums, comme l'âme des autres hommes voltige sur la musique!' The mouth is arched and refined by the mind, and at the moment is of the delicate tint that reminds one of the royal beauty of freshly plucked fruit. The chin is rounded, but nevertheless haughty and powerful as that of Balzac. The whole face is of a warm pallor, under which the rose tints of beautiful rich blood appear. A newly grown beard, like that of a young god, decorates it. The forehead, high and broad, magnificently drawn, is ornamented by black, thick hair, naturally wavy and curly like that of Paganini, which falls over a throat worthy of Achilles or Antinous."

One must not take this portrait too literally. It is seen through the medium of painting and poetry, and embellished by a certain idealisation. Still, it is no less sincere and faithful of Baudelaire as he appeared at that time. Charles Baudelaire had his hour of supreme beauty and perfect expansion, and we relate it after this faithful witness. It is rare that a poet, an artist, is known in the spring-time of his charm.

Reputation generally comes later, when the fatigue of study, the struggles of life, and the torture of passion have taken away youthfulness, leaving only the mask, faded and altered, on which each sorrow has made her impress. It is this last picture, which also has beauty, that one remembers. With his evasive singularity was mingled a certain exotic odour like the distant perfume of a country well loved of the sun. It is said that Baudelaire travelled for some time in India, and this fact explains much.

Contrary to the somewhat loose manners of artists generally, Baudelaire prided himself upon observing the most rigid *convenances*; his courtesy was often excessive to the point of affectation. He measured his phrases, using only the most carefully selected terms, and pronounced certain words in a particular manner, as though he wished to underline them and give them a mysterious signification. Italics and capital letters seemed to be marked in his voice.

Exaggeration, much in honour at Pimodan's, he disdained as theatrical and coarse, though he allowed himself the use of paradox. With a very simple, natural, and perfectly detached air, as though retailing, *à la* Prudhomme, a newspaper paragraph on the state of the weather, he would advance monstrous axioms, or uphold with perfect sang-froid some theory of mathematical extravagance; for he had method in the development of his follies. His spirit was neither in words nor traits; he saw things from a particular point of view which changed their outlines, as objects seen in a bird's-eye view are changed from when seen at their own elevation; he perceived analogies, inappreciable to others, the fantastic logic of which was very striking.

His gestures were slow, sober, and rare; for he held southern gesticulation in horror. Neither did he like volubility of speech, and British reserve appealed to his sense of good form. One might describe him as a dandy strayed into Bohemia; but preserving there his rank, and that cult of self which characterises a man imbued with the principles of Brummel.

Such was our impression of Baudelaire at our first meeting, the memory of which is as vivid as though it had occurred yesterday.

We were in the big salon, decorated in the style of Louis XIV, the wainscot enriched and set off with dull gold of a perfect tone, projecting cornices, on which some pupil of Lesueur or of Poussin, having studied at the Hôtel Lambert, had painted nymphs chased by satyrs through reed-grass, according to the mythological taste of the period. On the great marble chimney, veined with vermilion and white, was placed, in the guise of a clock, a golden elephant, harnessed like the elephant of Porus in the battle of Lebrun, supporting on its back a tower with an inscribed dial-plate. The chairs and settees were old and covered with faded tapestry, representing subjects of the chase by Oudry and Desportes.

It was in this salon, also, that the séances of the club of hashish-eaters took place, a club to which we belonged, the ecstasies, dreams, hallucinations of which, followed by the deepest dejection, we have described.

As was said above, the owner of this apartment was Fernand Boissard, whose short, curly, fair hair, white and vermilion complexion, grey eyes scintillating with light and *esprit*, red lips and pearly teeth, seemed to witness to the health and exuberance of a Rubens, and to promise a life more than usually long. But, alas, who is able to foresee the fate of another? Boissard, to whom none of the conditions of happiness were lacking, fell a victim to a malady much the same as that which caused the death of Baudelaire.

No one was better equipped than Boissard. He had the most open-minded intelligence; he understood painting, poetry, and music equally well; but, in him, the dilettante was stronger than the artist. Admiration took up too much of his time; he exhausted himself in his enthusiasms. There is no doubt that, had necessity with her iron hand compelled him, he would have been an excellent painter. The success that was obtained by the "Episode de la retraite de Russie" would have been his sure guarantee. But, without abandoning painting, he allowed himself to be diverted by other arts. He played the violin, organised quartettes, studied Bach, Beethoven, Meyerbeer, and Mendelssohn, learnt languages, wrote criticisms, and composed some charming sonnets.

He was a voluptuary in Art, and no one enjoyed real masterpieces with more refinement, passion, and sensuousness than he did. From force of admiring, he forgot to express beauty, and what he felt so deeply he came to believe he had created. His conversation was charming, full of gaiety and originality. He had a rare gift of inventing words and phrases, and all sorts of bizarre expressions, that linger in the mind.

Like Baudelaire, amorous of new and rare sensations, even when they were dangerous, he wished to know those artificial paradises, which, later, made him pay so dearly for their transient ecstasies. It was the abuse of hashish that, undoubtedly, undermined his constitution, formerly so robust and strong.

This souvenir of a friend of our youth, with whom we lived under the same roof, of a romantic to whom fame did not come because he loved too much the work of others to dream of his own, will not be out of place here, in this introduction destined to serve as a preface to the complete works of a departed friend of us both.

On the day of our visit Jean Feuchères, the sculptor, was there. Besides his talent in statuary, Feuchères had a remarkable power of imitation, such as no actor was able to compass. He was the inventor of the comic dialogues between Sergeant Bridais and gunner Pitou, which even to-day provoke irresistible laughter. Feuchères died first, and, of the four artists assembled on that day at the Hôtel Pimodan, we only survive.

On the sofa, half recumbent, her elbow resting on a cushion, with an immobility of pose she often assumed, Maryx listened dreamily to Baudelaire's paradoxes. No surprise was manifested on her almost Oriental countenance. She wore a white robe, oddly ornamented with red spots like tiny drops of blood, and while Baudelaire talked she lazily passed the rings from one hand to another – hands as perfect as was her figure.

Near the window, the "Femme au serpent" (it is not permitted to give her name) having thrown back her lace wrap and delicate little green hood, such as never adorned Lucy Hocquet or Madame Baurand, over an arm-chair, shook out her beautiful fawn-brown hair, for she had come from the Swimming Baths, and, her person all draped in muslin, exhaled, like a naiad, the fragrant perfume of the bath. With her eyes and smile she encouraged this tilt of words, and threw in, now and again, her own remarks, sometimes mocking, sometimes appreciative.

They have passed, those charming leisure hours, when poets, artists, and beautiful women were gathered together to talk of Art, literature, and love, as the century of Boccaccio has passed. Time, Death, the imperious necessities of life, have dispersed this mutually sympathetic group; but the memory is dear to all those who had the good fortune to be admitted to it. It is not without an involuntary sigh that these lines are penned.

Shortly after this first meeting Baudelaire came to see us and brought a volume of his verses. He himself relates this visit in a literary article which he wrote about us in terms of such admiration that we dare not transcribe them.

From that moment a friendship was formed between us, in which Baudelaire always wished to conserve the attitude of favourite disciple to a sympathetic master, although he owed his success only to himself and his own originality. Never in our greatest familiarity did he relax that deference of manner which to us seemed excessive and with which we would gladly have dispensed. He acknowledged it *à vive voix*, and the dedication of the "Flowers of Evil" which is addressed to us, consecrates in its lapidary form the absolute expression of his loving and poetical devotion.

If we insist on these details, it is not for their actual worth, but solely because they portray an unrecognised side of Baudelaire's character.

This poet, whom people try to describe as of so satanic a nature, smitten with evil and depravity (literary, be it well understood), knew love and admiration in the highest degree.

But the distinguishing feature of Satan is that he is incapable of admiration or love. The light wounds him, glory is a sight insupportable to him, and makes him want to veil his eyes with his bat-like wings. No one, even at the time of fervour for romanticism, had more respect and adoration for the great masters than Baudelaire. He was always ready to pay his legitimate tribute of praise to those who merited it, and that without the servility of a disciple, without fanaticism; for he himself was a master, having his realm, his subjects, and his coinage of gold.

It would perhaps be fitting, after having portrayed Baudelaire in all the freshness of his youth and in the fulness of his power, to present him as he was during the later years of his life, before Death stretched out his hand towards him, and sealed the lips which will no longer speak here below. His face was thin and spiritualised; the eyes seemed larger, the nose thinner; the lips were closed mysteriously, and seemed to guard ironical secrets. The vermilion tints of the past had given place to a swarthy, tired yellow. As to the forehead, it had gained in grandeur and solidity – so to speak; one would have said that it was carved in some particularly durable marble. The fine hair, silky and long, nearly white, falling round a face which was young and old at the same time, gave him an almost sacerdotal appearance.

Charles Baudelaire was born in Paris on April 21st, 1821, in an old turreted house, in the Rue Hautefeuille. He was the son of M. Baudelaire, the old friend of Condorcet and of Cabanis, a distinguished and well-educated man who retained the polished manners of the eighteenth century, which the pretentious tastes of the Republican era had not so entirely effaced as is sometimes thought. This characteristic was strong in the poet, who always retained the outward forms of courtesy.

In his young days Baudelaire was in no way out of the

ordinary, and neither did he gain many laurels at his college prize distributions. He even found the B.A. examination a great difficulty, and his degree was honorary. Troubled by abstract questions, this boy, so fine of spirit and keen of intelligence, appeared almost like an idiot. We have no intention of declaring this inaptitude as a sign of cleverness; but, under the eye of the pedagogue, often distrait and idle, or rather preoccupied, the real man is formed little by little, unperceived by masters or parents.

M. Baudelaire died, and his wife, Charles's mother, married General Aupick, who became Ambassador to Constantinople. Dissension soon arose in the family à propos of young Baudelaire's desire for a literary career. We think it wrong to reproach parents with the fears they manifest when the gift of poetry develops in their offspring. Alas! They are right. To what sad, precarious, and miserable existence does he vow himself – he who takes up a literary career? From that day he must consider himself cut off from human beings, active life; he no longer lives – he is the spectator of life. All sensation comes to him as motif for analysis. Involuntarily he develops two distinct personalities, and, lacking other subjects, one becomes the spy on the other. If he lack a corpse, he stretches himself on the slab of black marble and buries the scalpel deep in his own heart. And what desperate struggles must he endure with the Idea, that elusive Proteus, who takes all manner of forms to escape captivity, and who will only deliver his oracle when he has been forced to show himself in his true aspect! This Idea, when one holds it, frightened, trembling, vanquished, one must nourish, clothe, fold round in that robe so difficult to weave, to colour and to arrange in graceful curves. During this long-drawn-out task the nerves become irritable, the brain on fire, the sensibilities quickened, and then nervous disorder comes with all its odd anxieties, its unconscious hallucinations, its indefinable sufferings, its morbid capriciousness, its fantastic depravity, its infatuations and motiveless dislikes, its mad energy and nervous prostration, its searches for excitement and its disgust for all healthy nourishment.

We do not exaggerate the picture; but we have before us only the talented poets, crowned with glory, who have, at the last, succumbed on the breast of their ideal. What would it be if we went down into the Limbo where the shades of still-born children are wailing, like those abortive endeavours and larvæ of thought which can achieve neither wing nor form? Yes! Desire is not power, nor is Love possession!

Faith is not enough. Another gift is necessary.

In literature, as in religion, work without grace is futile.

Although they do not suspect this region of anguish, for, to know it really, it is necessary to go down oneself, not under the guidance of a Vergil or a Dante, but under that of a Lousteau, of a Lucien de Rubempré, parents instinctively display the perils and suffering of the artistic life in the endeavour to dissuade the children they love, and for for whom they desire one more happy and ordinarily human.

Once only since the earth has revolved round the sun have parents ardently wished to have a son's life dedicated to poetry. The child received the most brilliant literary education, and, with the irony of Fate, became Chapelain, the author of "La Pucelle"! and this, one might even say, was to play with sinister fortune!

To turn his stubborn ideas into another course, Baudelaire was made to travel. He was sent a great distance, embarking on a vessel, the captain of which took him to the Indian seas. He visited the Isles of Mauritius, Bourbon, Madagascar, Ceylon perhaps, and some parts of the "Isle of the Ganges"; but he would not, for all that, give up his intention of becoming a man of letters. They tried vainly to interest him in commerce, but a trade in cattle to feed Anglo-Indians on beefsteak had no attractions for him. All he retained of this voyage was a memory of great splendour which remained with him all his life. He gloried in a sky where brilliant constellations, unknown in Europe, were to be found; the magnificent vegetation with the exotic perfumes, the elegantly odd pagodas, the brown faces and the soft white draperies – all that in Nature was so warm, powerful, and full of colour.

In his verses he was frequently led from the mists and mud of Paris to the countries of light, azure, and perfume. Between the lines of the most sombre of his poems, a window is opened through which can be seen, instead of the black chimneys and smoky roofs, the blue Indian seas, or a beach of golden sand on which the slender figure of a Malabaraise, half naked, carrying an amphora on the head, is running. Without penetrating too deeply into the private life of the poet, one can imagine that it was during this voyage that Baudelaire fell in love with the "Venus noire," of whom he was a worshipper all his life.

When he returned from his distant travels he had just attained his majority; there was no longer any reason – not even financial, for he was rich for some time at least – to oppose Baudelaire's choice of a vocation; it was only strengthened by meeting with obstacles, and nothing would deter him.

Lodged in a little apartment under the roof of the same Hôtel Pimodan where later we met him, as has been related earlier in this introduction, he commenced that life of work, interrupted and resumed, of varied studies, of fruitful idleness, which is that of each man of letters seeking his particular field of labour. Baudelaire soon found his. He conceived something beyond romanticism – a land unexplored, a sort of rough and wild Kamtschatka; and it was at the extreme verge that he built for himself, as Sainte-Beuve, who thoroughly appreciated him, said, a kiosque of bizarre architecture.

Several of the poems which are to be found amongst the "Flowers of Evil" were already composed. Baudelaire, like all born poets, from the start possessed a form and style of which he was master; it was more accentuated and polished later, but still the same. Baudelaire has often been accused of studied bizarrerie, of affected and laboured originality, and especially of manner- isms. This is a point at which it is necessary to pause before going further. There are people who have naturally an affected manner. In them simplicity would be pure affectation, a sort of inverted mannerism. Long practice is necessary to be naturally simple. The circumvolutions of the brain twist themselves in such a manner that the ideas get entangled and confused and go up in spirals instead of following straight lines. The most complicated, subtle, and intense thoughts are those which present themselves first. They see things from a peculiar angle which alters the aspect and perspective. All fancies, the most odd, unusual, and fantastically distant from the subject treated of, strike them chiefly, and they know how to draw them into their woof by mysterious threads.

Baudelaire had a brain like this, and where the critic has tried to see labour, effort, excess, there is only the free and easy manifestation of individuality. These poems, of a savour so exquisitely strange, cost him no more than any badly rhymed commonplace.

Baudelaire, always possessed of great admiration for the old masters, never felt it incumbent upon him to take them for models; they had had the good fortune to arrive in the early days of the world, at the dawn, so to speak, of humanity, when nothing had been expressed yet, and each form, each image, each sentiment, had the charm of virginal novelty. The great commonplaces which form the foundation of human thought were then in all their glory and sufficed for simple geniuses, speaking to simple people.

But, from force of repetition, these general subjects of verse were used up like money which, from continual circulation, has lost its imprint; and, besides, Life had become more complex, fuller of originality, and could no longer be represented in the artificial spirit of another age.

As true innocence charms, so the trickery of pretended innocence disgusts and displeases. The quality of the nineteenth century is not precisely naïveté, and it needs, to render its thoughts and dreams explicit, idiom a little more composite than that employed in the classics. Literature is like a day; it has its morning, noon, evening, and night. Without vain expatiation as to whether one should prefer dawn or twilight, one ought to paint the hour which is at hand, and with a palette of all the colours necessary to give it its full effect. Has not sunset its beauty as well as dawn? The copper-reds, the bronze-golds, the turquoise melting to sapphire, all the tints which blend and pass away in the great final conflagration, the light-pierced clouds which seem to take the form of a falling aerial Babel – have they not as much to offer to the poet as the rosy-fingered Dawn? But the time when the Hours preceded the Chariot of Day is long since fled.

The poet of the "Flowers of Evil" loved what is unwisely known as the style of the decadence, and which is no other thing than Art arrived at that point of extreme maturity that determines civilisations which have grown old; ingenious, complicated, clever, full of delicate tints and refinements, gathering all the delicacies of speech, borrowing from technical vocabularies, taking colour from every palette, tones from all musical instruments, forcing itself to the expression of the most elusive thoughts, contours vague and fleeting, listening to translate subtle confidences, confessions of depraved passions and the odd hallucinations of a fixed idea turning to madness.

This style of the decadence is the "dernier mot" of Verbe, summoned to express all and to venture to the very extremes. One can recall, à propos of him, language already veined with the greenness of decomposition, savouring of the Lower Roman Empire and the complicated refinements of the Byzantine School, the last form of Greek Art fallen into deliquescence; but such is the necessary and fatal idiom of peoples and civilisations where an artificial life has replaced a natural one and developed in a man who does not know his own needs. It is not easy, moreover, this style condemned by pedants, for it expresses new ideas in new forms and words that have never been heard of before. Contrary to the classical style, it admits of backgrounds where the spectres of superstition, the haggard phantoms of dreams, the terrors of night, remorse which leaps out and falls back noiselessly, obscure fantasies that astonish the day, and all that the soul in its deepest depths and innermost caverns conceals of darkness, deformity, and horror, move together confusedly. One can well imagine that the fourteen hundred words of the dialect of Racine do not suffice an author who is given the difficult task of rendering modern ideas and things in all their infinite complexity and their diversity of colour.

Thus Baudelaire, who, despite his ill success at his baccalaureate examination, was a good Latinist, preferred undoubtedly, to Vergil and to Cicero, Apuleius, Juvenal, Saint Augustine, and Tertullian, whose style has the black radiance of ebony. He went even to the Latin of the Church, to hymns and chants in which the rhyme represents the old forgotten rhythm, and he has addressed, under the title of "Franciscæ meæ Laudes," "To an erudite and devotee," such are the terms of the dedication, a Latin poem rhymed in the form that Brizeux called ternary, which is composed of three rhymes following one another, instead e of alternating as in the tiercet of Dante. To this odd piece of work is joined a note no less singular. We transcribe it here, for it explains and corroborates what has just been said about the idioms of the decadence:

"Does it not seem to the reader, as to me, that the language of the last Latin decadence – the supreme sigh of the strong man already transformed and prepared for the spiritual life – is singularly adequate to express the passion that is comprised in, and felt by, the modern world? Mysticism is the opposite pole on the compass of Catullus and his followers, purely cynical and superficial poets, who have only known the pole of sensuality. In this marvellous language, solecism and barbarism seem to me to express the negligences of a passion forgetful of itself and regardless of conventionality. The words, taken in a new acceptation, reveal the charming maladroitness of a northern barbarian kneeling before a Roman beauty. The pun itself, when it crosses pedantism, has it not the saving grace and irregularity of infancy?"

It is unnecessary to push this point further. Baudelaire, when he had not to express some curious deviation, some unknown side of the soul, employed pure, clear language, so correct and exact that even the most difficult to please would find nothing to complain of. This is especially noticeable in his prose writings, when he treats of more general and less abstruse subjects than in his verse.

With regard to his philosophical and literary tenets, they were those of Edgar Allan Poe, whom he had not then translated but whom he greatly admired. One can apply to him the phrases that he himself wrote of the American author in the preface to the "Extraordinary Histories ": – "He considered progress, the great modern idea, as the ecstasy of fools, and he called the perfect-ionings of human habitations, scars and rectangular abominations. He believed only in the Immutable, the Eternal, the self-same, and he was in the possession of – cruel privilege! in a society amorous only of itself – the great good sense of a Machiavelli who marches before the wise as a column of light across the desert of history." Baudelaire had a perfect horror of philanthropists, progressionists, utilitarians, humanitarians, Utopians, and of all those who pretend to reform things, contrary to nature and the universal laws of society. He desired neither the suppression of hell nor of the guillotine for the disposal of sinners and assassins. He did not believe that men were born good, and he admitted original perversity as an element to be found in the depths of the purest souls – perversity, that evil counsellor who leads a man on to do what is fatal to himself, precisely because it is fatal and for the pleasure of acting contrary to law, without other attraction than disobedience, outside of sensuality, profit, or charm. This perversity he believes to be in others as in himself; therefore, when he finds a servant in fault he refrains from scolding him, for he regards it as an irremediable curse. It is, then, very wrong of short-sighted critics to have accused Baudelaire of immorality, an easy form of evil-speaking for the mediocre and the jealous, and always well taken up by the Pharisees and J. Prudhommes. No one has professed greater disgust for baseness of mind or unseemliness of subject.

He hated evil as a mathematical deviation, and, in his quality of a perfect gentleman, he scorned it as unseemly, ridiculous, bourgeois and squalid. If he has often treated of hideous, repugnant, and unhealthy subjects, it is from that horror and fascination which makes the magnetised bird go down into the unclean mouth of the serpent; but more than once, with a vigorous flap of his wings, he breaks the charm and flies upwards to bluer and more spiritual regions. He should have engraved on his seal as a device the words "Spleen et Idéal," which form the title of the first part of his book of verse.

If his bouquet is composed of strange flowers, of metallic colourings and exotic perfumes, the calyx of which, instead of joy contains bitter tears and drops of aqua-tofana, he can reply that he planted but a few into the black soil, saturating them in putre-faction, as the soil of a cemetery dissolves the corpses of preceding centuries among mephitic miasmas. Undoubtedly roses, marguerites, violets, are the more agreeable spring flowers; but he thinks little of them in the black mud with which the pavements of the town are covered. And, moreover, Baudelaire, if he understands the great tropical landscapes where, as in dreams, trees burst forth in strange and gigantic elegance, is only little touched by the small rural sites on the outskirts; and it is not he who will frolic like the Philistines of Heinrich Heine before the romantic efflorescence of spring and faint away at the song of the sparrows. He likes to follow the pale, shrivelled, contorted man, convulsed by passions, and actual modern ennui, through the sinuosities of that great madrepore of Paris – to surprise him in his difficulties, agonies, miseries, prostrations, and excitements, his nervousness and despair.

He watches the budding of evil instincts, the ignoble habits idly acquired in degradation. And, from this sight which attracts and repels him, he becomes incurably melancholy; for he thinks himself no better than others, and allows the pure arc of the heavens and the brilliancy of the stars to be veiled by impure mists.

With these ideas one can well understand that Baudelaire

believed in the absolute self-government of Art, and that he would not admit that poetry should have any end outside itself, or any mission to fulfil other than that of exciting in the soul of the reader the sensation of supreme beauty – beauty in the absolute sense of the term. To this sensation he liked to add a certain effect of surprise, astonishment, and rarity. As much as possible he banished from poetry a too realistic imitation of eloquence, passion, and a too exact truth. As in statuary one does not mould forms directly after Nature, so he wished that, before entering the sphere of Art, each object should be subjected to a metamorphosis that would adapt it to this subtle medium, idealising it and abstracting it from trivial reality.

Such principles are apt to astonish us, when we read certain of the poems of Baudelaire in which horror seems to be sought like pleasure; but that we should not be deceived, this horror is always transfigured by character and effect, by a ray of Rembrandt, or a trait of Velasquez, who portrayed the race under sordid deformity. In stirring up in his cauldron all sorts of fantastically odd and enormous ingredients, Baudelaire can say, with the witches of Macbeth, "Fair is foul, and foul is fair." This sort of intentional ugliness is not, then, in contradiction to the supreme aim of Art; and the poems, such as the "Sept Vieillards" and the "Petits Vieilles," have snatched from the poetical Saint John who dreams in Patmos this phrase, which characterises so well the author of the "Flowers of Evil": "You have endowed the sky of Art with one knows not what macabre ray; you have created a new *frisson*."

But it is, so to speak, only the shadow of the talent of Baudelaire, a shadow ardently fiery or coldly blue, which allows him to give the essential and luminous touch. There is a serenity in his nervous, febrile, and tormenting talent. On the highest summits he is tranquil: *pacem summa tenent.*

But, instead of writing of the poet's ideas, it would be infinitely better to allow him to speak for himself: "Poetry, little as one wishes to penetrate one's self, to question one's soul, to recall the memories of past enthusiasm, has no other end than itself; it cannot have any other, and no poem will be so great, so noble, so truly worthy of the name of poem, as that which is written purely from the pleasure of writing.

"I do not say that poetry does not ennoble tastes – be it well understood – that its final result is not to raise men above vulgar interests. This would be an obvious absurdity. I say that, if the poet has followed a moral aim, he has diminished his poetical power, and it would not be imprudent to lay a wager that his work will be bad. Poetry is unable, under pain of death or decay, to assimilate itself to morals or science.

"It has not Truth as an object; it has Itself. The demonstration of Truth is elsewhere.

"Truth has only to do with songs; all that gives charm and grace to a song will give to Truth its authority and power. Coldness, calmness, impassivity, drive back the diamonds and flowers of the Muse; they are absolutely in opposition to poetical humour.

"The Pure Intellect aspires to Truth, Taste informs us of Beauty, and Moral Sense teaches us Duty. It is true that the middle sense is intimately connected with the other two, and is only separated from the Moral Sense by very slight divergences, so that Aristotle has not hesitated to place some of its operations among the virtues themselves. Also, that which especially exasperates the man of Taste in the sight of Vice is its deformity and disproportion. Vice outrages justice and truth, revolts the Intellect and Conscience; but, like an outrage in harmony – a dissonance – it wounds more particularly certain poetical natures, and I do not believe it would be scandalous to consider all infraction of moral, the beautiful moral, as a fault against rhythm and universal prosody.

"It is this admirable, this immortal instinct of Beauty which makes us consider the earth and all its manifold forms, sounds, odours, sentiments, as a hint of, and correspondence to, Heaven. The insatiable thirst for that which is beyond and which veils life, is the most lively proof of our immortality. It is at once by and through poetry, by and through music, that the soul gets a glimpse of the splendours beyond the tomb. And, when an exquisite poem brings tears to the eyes, these tears are not the proof of an excess of joy, they are the witness rather of an excited melancholy, an intercession of the nerves, of a nature exiled in imperfection wishing to possess itself, even on this earth, of a revealed paradise.

"Thus, the principle of poetry is, strictly and simply, the Human Aspiration towards Supreme Beauty; and the manifestation of this principle is in the enthusiasm, the awakening of the soul, enthusiasm quite independent of that passion, which is the intoxication of the heart, and of that Truth, which is the Food of Reason. For passion is a natural thing, too natural even not to introduce a wounding note, discordant in the domain of un-sullied Beauty; too familiar and too violent not to degrade pure Desires, gracious Melancholies and noble Despairs, which inhabit the supernatural regions of Poetry."

Although few poets have a more spontaneously sparkling inspiration and originality than Baudelaire – doubtless through distaste for the false poetic style which affects to believe in the descent of a tongue of fire on the writer painfully rhyming a strophe – he pretended that the true author provoked, directed, and modified at will this mysterious power of literary production; and we find in a very curious piece which precedes the translation of Edgar Poe's celebrated poem "The Raven," the following lines, half ironical, half serious, in which Baudelaire's own opinion is set down under the guise of an analysis of the famous American author:

"The poetic principle, which makes the rules of poetry, is formulated, it is said, and modelled after the poems. Here is a poet who pretends that his poems have been composed according to technique or principle. He had certainly great genius and more inspiration than is general, if by inspiration one understands energy, intellectual enthusiasm, and the power of keeping all his faculties on the alert. He loved work more than anything else; he liked to repeat, he, the finished original, that originality is something needing apprenticeship, which does not necessarily mean to say that it is a thing to be transmitted by instruction. Chance and incomprehensibility were his two great enemies. Has he willingly diminished that faculty which was in him to take the most beautiful part? I should be inclined to think so; however, one must not forget that his genius, so ardent and agile, was passionately fond of analysis, combination, and calculation. One of his favourite axioms was the following: 'Everything in a poem as in a novel, everything in a sonnet as in a novelette, ought to contribute to the *dénouement*. A good writer has the last line already in his mind when he writes the first.'

"Owing to this admirable method the writer was able to begin even at the end, and work, when it pleased him, at whatever part he liked. Amateurs will perhaps sneer at these cynical maxims, but each can learn from them what he wishes. It would be useless to show them what Art has gained from deliberation, and to make clear to the world what exacting labour this object of luxury known as poetry really is. After all, a little charlatanry is permitted to genius. It is like the paint on the cheeks of a naturally beautiful woman, a new condition of the mind."

This last phrase is characteristic and betrays the individual taste of the poet for artificiality. He, moreover, does not hide this predilection. He takes pleasure in this kind of composite beauty, and now and then a little artificiality that elaborates advanced and unsound civilisations. Let us say, to take a concrete example, that he would prefer to a simple young girl who used no other cosmetic than water, a more mature woman employing all the resources of the accomplished coquette, in front of a dressing-table covered with bottles of essences, *de lait virginal*, ivory brushes, and curling-tongs. The sweet perfume of skin macerated in aromatics, like that of Esther, who was steeped in oil of palms for six months and six months in cinnamon, before presentation to

King Ahasuerus, had on him a powerful effect. A light touch of rose or hortensia on a fresh cheek, beauty-spots carefully and provocatively placed at the corner of the mouth or of the eye, eye-lashes burnished with kohl, hair tinted with russet-brown and powdered with gold-dust, neck and shoulders whitened with rice-powder, lips and the tips of the fingers brightened with carmine, did not in any way revolt him.

He liked these touches of Art upon Nature, the high lights, the strong lights placed by a clever hand to augment grace, charm and the character of the face. It is not he who would write virtuous tirades against painting, rougeing, and the crinoline. All that removed a man, and especially a woman, from the natural state found favour in his eyes. These tastes explain themselves and ought to be understandable in a poet of the decadence, and the author of the "Flowers of Evil."

We shall astonish no one if we add that he preferred, to the simple perfume of the rose or violet, that of benzoin, amber, and even musk, so little appreciated in our days, and also the penetrating aroma of certain exotic flowers the perfume of which is too strong for our moderate climate. Baudelaire had, in the matter of perfumes, a strangely subtle sensuality which is rarely to be met with except amongst Orientals. He sought it always, and the phrase cited by Banville and at the commencement of this article may very justly be said of him: "Mon âme voltige sur les parfums comme l'âme des autres hommes voltige sur la musique."

He loved also toilets of a bizarre elegance, a capricious richness, striking fantasy, in which something of the comedian and courtesan was mingled, although he himself was severely conventional in dress; but this taste, excessive, singular, anti-natural, nearly always opposed to classical beauty, was for him the sign of the human will correcting, to its taste, the forms and colours furnished by matter.

Where the philosopher could only find a text for declamation he found a proof of grandeur. Depravity – that is to say, a step aside from the normal type – is impossible to the stupid. It is for the same reason that inspired poets, not having the control and direction of their works, caused him a sort of aversion, and why he wished to introduce art and technique even into originality.

So much for the metaphysical; but Baudelaire was of a subtle, complicated, reasoning, and paradoxical nature, and had more philosophy than is general amongst poets. The æsthetics of his art occupied him much; he abounded in systems which he tried to realise, and all that he did was first planned out. According to him, literature ought to be *intentional*, and the *accidental* restrained as much as possible. This, however, did not prevent him, in true poetical fashion, from profiting by the happy chances of executing those beauties which burst forth suddenly without premeditation, like the little flowers accidentally mixed with the grain chosen by the sower. Every artist is somewhat like Lope de Vega, who, at the moment of the composition of his comedies, locked up his precepts under six keys – *con seis claves*. In the ardour of his work, voluntarily or not, he forgot systems and paradoxes.

II

Baudelaire's reputation, which during some years had not extended beyond the limits of the little circle who rallied round the new poet, widened suddenly when he presented himself to the public holding in his hand the bouquet of the "Flowers of Evil," a bouquet which in no way resembled the innocent posy of the débutante. Some of the poems were so subtly suggestive, yet so abstruse and enveloped with the forms and veils of Art, that the authorities demanded that they should be withdrawn and replaced by others of less dangerous eccentricity, before the book could be comprised in libraries. Ordinarily, there is no great excitement about a book of verses; they are born, live, and die in silence; for two or three poets suffice for our intellectual consummation.

In the excitement, rumour, and allayed scandal which surrounded Baudelaire, it was recognised that he had given the public, which is a rare occurrence, original work of a peculiar savour. To create in the public a new sensation is the greatest joy that can happen to a writer, and especially to a poet.

"Flowers of Evil" was one of those happy titles that are more difficult to find than is generally imagined. He summed up in a brief and poetical form the general idea of the book and indicated its tendencies. Although it was evidently romantic in intention and composition, it was impossible, by even ever so frail a thread, to connect Baudelaire with any one of the great masters of that particular school. His verses, refined and subtle in structure, encasing the subjects dealt with so closely as to resemble armour rather than clothing, at first appeared difficult and obscure. This feeling was caused, not through any fault of the author, but from the novelty of the things he expressed – things that had not before been made vocal. It was part of Baudelaire's doctrine that, to attain his end, a poet must invent language and rhythm for himself. But he could not prevent surprise on the part of the reader when confronted with verse so different from any he had read before. In painting the evils which horrified him, Baudelaire knew how to find the morbidly rich tints of decomposition, the tones of mother-of-pearl which freeze stagnant waters, the roses of consumption, the pallor of chlorosis, the hateful bilious yellows, the leaden grey of pestilential fogs, the poisoned and metallic greens smelling of sulphide of arsenic, the blackness of smoke diluted by the rain on plaster walls, the bitumens baked and browned in the depths of hell; and all that gamut of intensified colours, correspondent to autumn, to the setting of the sun, to over-ripe fruit, and the last hours of civilisation.

The book is opened by a poem to the reader, whom the poet does not attempt to cajole, as is usual, and to whom he tells the absolute truth. He accuses him, in spite of all his hypocrisy, of having the vices for which he blames others, and of nourishing in his own heart that great modern monster, Ennui, who, with his bourgeois cowardice, dreams of the ferocity and debauches of the Romans, of bureaucrat Nero, and shop-keeper Heliogabalus.

One other poem, of great beauty, and entitled, undoubtedly by an ironical antiphrasis, "Benediction," depicts the coming of the poet to the world, an object of astonishment and aversion to his mother as a shameful offspring. We see him pursued by stupidity, envy, and sarcasm, a prey to the perfidious cruelty of some Delilah, happy in delivering him up to the Philistines, naked, disarmed, after having expended on him all the refinements of a ferocious coquetry. Then there is his arrival, after insults, miseries, tortures, purified in the crucible of sorrow, to eternal glory, to the crown of light destined for the heads of the martyrs who have suffered for Truth and Beauty.

One little poem which follows later, and which is entitled "Soleil," closes with a sort of tacit justification of the poet in his vagrant courses. A bright ray shines on the muddy town; the author is going out and runs through the unclean streets, the by-ways where the closed shutters hide indications of secret luxuries; all the black, damp, dirty labyrinths of old streets to the houses of the blind and leprous, where the light shines here and there on some window, on a pot of flowers, or on the head of a young girl. Is not the poet like the sun which alone enters everywhere, in the hospital as in the palace, in the hovel as in the church, always divine, letting his golden radiance fall on the carrion or on the rose?

"Élévation" shows us the poet floating in the sky, beyond the starry spheres; in the luminous ether; on the confines of our universe; disappearing into the depths of infinity like a tiny cloud; intoxicating himself with that rare and salubrious air where there are none of the miasmas pertaining to the earth and only the pure ether breathed by the angels. We must not forget that Baudelaire, although he has often been accused of materialism, and reproached for expending his talent upon doubtful subjects, is, on the contrary, endowed in a large degree with the great gift of spirituality, as Swedenborg said. He also possesses the power of correspondence, to employ a mystical idiom; that is to say, he knows how to discover by secret intuition the unexpressed feelings of others, and how to approach them, by those unexpected analogies that only the far-sighted are able to seize upon. Each poet has this power more or less developed, which is the very essence of his art.

Undoubtedly Baudelaire, in this book dedicated to the painting of depravity and modern perversity, has framed repugnant pictures, where vice is laid bare to wallow in all the ugliness of its shame; but the poet, with supreme contempt, scornful indignation, and a constant recurrence towards the ideal which is so often lacking in satirical writers, stigmatises and marks with an indelible red iron the unhealthy flesh, plastered with unguents and white lead.

In no part is the thirst for pure air, the immaculate whiteness of the Himalayan snows, the azure without blot, the unfading light, more strong and ardent than in the poems that have been termed *immoral*, as if the flagellation of vice was vice itself, and as if one is a poisoner for having written of the poisonous pharmacy of the Borgia. This method is by no means new, but it thrives always, and certain people pretend to believe that one cannot read the "Flowers of Evil" except with a glass mask, such as Exili wore when he worked at the famous powder of succession.

We have read Baudelaire's poems often, and we are not struck dead with convulsed face and blackened body, as though we had supped with Vanozza in a vineyard of Pope Alexander VI. All such foolishness – unfortunately detrimental, for all the fools enthusiastically adopt that attitude – would make any artist worthy of the name but shrug his shoulders when told that blue is moral and scarlet immoral. It is rather as if one said: "The potato is virtuous, henbane is criminal."

A charming poem on perfumes classifies them, rousing ideas, sensations, and memories. Some are fresh, like the flesh of an infant, green like the fields in spring, recalling the blush of dawn and carrying with them the thoughts of innocence. Others, like musk, amber, benzoin, nard, and incense, are superb, triumphant, worldly, and provoke coquetry, love, luxury, festivities, and splendours. If one transposed them into the sphere of colours, they would represent gold and purple. The poet often recurs to this idea of the significance of perfumes. Surrounding a tawny beauty from the Cape, who seemed to have a mission for sleeping off home sickness, he spoke of this mixed odour "of musk and havana" which transported her soul to the well-loved lands of the Sun, where the leaves of the palm-trees make fans in the blue and tepid air, where the masts of the ships sway harmoniously to the roll of the sea, while the silent slaves try to distract their young master from his languishing melancholy. Further on, wondering what will remain of his work, he compares himself to an old flagon, forgotten amongst the spider-webs, at the bottom of some cupboard in a deserted house.

From the open cupboard comes the mustiness of the past, feeble perfumes of robes, laces, powder-boxes, which revive memories of old loves and antiquated elegance; and, if by chance one uncorks a rancid and sticky phial, an acrid smell of English salts and vinegar escapes, a powerful antidote to the modern pestilence.

In many à passage this preoccupation with aroma appears, surrounding with a subtle cloud all persons and things. In very few of the poets do we find this care. Generally they are content with putting light, colour, and music in their verses; but it is rare that they pour in that drop of pure essence with which Baudelaire's muse never failed to moisten the sponge or the cambric of his handkerchief.

Since we are recounting the individual likings and minor passions of the poet, let us say that he adored cats – like him, amorous of perfumes, and who are thrown into a sort of epileptical ecstasy by the scent of valerian. He loved these charming, tranquil, mysterious, gentle animals, with their electrical shudders, whose favourite attitude is the recumbent pose of the Sphinx, which seems to have passed on to them its secret. They ramble round the house with their velvet footfalls as the genius of the place – *genius loci* – or come and seat themselves on the table near the writer, keeping company with his thoughts and watching him from the depths of their sanded golden eyes with intelligent tenderness and magical penetration.

It is said that cats divine the thoughts which the brain transmits to the pen, and that, stretching out their paws, they wish to seize the written passage. They are happy in silence, order, and quietude, and no place suits them better than the study of a literary man. They wait patiently until his task is done, all the time purring gently and rhythmically in a sort of *sotto voce* accompaniment. Sometimes they gloss over with their tongue some disordered fur; for they are clean, careful, coquettish, and will not allow of any irregularity in their toilet, but all is done quietly and discreetly as though they feared to distract or hinder. Their caresses are tender, delicate, silent, *feminine*, having nothing in common with the clamorous, clumsy petulance that is found in dogs, to whom all the sympathy of the vulgar is given.

All these merits were appreciated by Baudelaire, who has more than once addressed beautiful poems to cats – the "Flowers of Evil" contain three – where he celebrates their physical and moral virtues, and often he makes them pass through his compositions as a sort of additional characteristic. Cats abound in Baudelaire's verse, as dogs in the pictures of Paul Veronese, and form there a kind of signature.

It also must be added that in these sweet animals there is a nocturnal side, mysterious and cabalistic, which was very attractive to the poet. The cat, with his phosphoric eyes, which are like lanterns and stars to him, fearlessly haunts the darkness, where he meets wandering phantoms, sorcerers, alchemists, necromancers, resurrectionists, lovers, pickpockets, assassins, grey patrols, and all the obscene spectres of the night. He has the appearance of knowing the latest sabbatical chronicle, and he will willingly rub himself against the lame leg of Mephistopheles. His nocturnal serenades, his loves on the tiles, accompanied by cries like those of a child being murdered, give him a certain satanical air which justifies up to a certain point the repugnance of diurnal and practical minds, for whom the mysteries of Erebus have not the slightest attraction. But a doctor Faustus, in his cell littered with books and instruments of alchemy, would love always to have a cat for a companion.

Baudelaire himself was a voluptuous, cajoling cat, with just its velvety manners, alluring mysteries, instinct with power concealed in suppleness, fixing on things and men his penetrating look, disquieting, eccentric, difficult to withstand, but faithful and without perfidy.

Many women pass through the poems of Baudelaire, some veiled, some half discernible, but to whom it is impossible to attribute names. They are rather types than individuals. They represent l'*éternel féminin*, and the love that the poet expresses for them is *the* love and not a love. We have seen that in his theories he did not admit of individual passion, finding it too masterful, too familiar and violent.

Among these women some symbolise unconscious and almost bestial prostitution, with plastered and painted masks, eyes brightened with kohl, mouths tinted with scarlet, seeming like open wounds, false hair and jewels; others, of a colder corruption, more clever and more perverse, like marchionesses of Marteuil of the nineteenth century, transpose the vice of the body to the soul. They are haughty, icy, bitter, finding pleasure only in wickedness; insatiable as sterility, mournful as ennui, having only hysterical and foolish fancies, and deprived, like the devil, of the power of love. Gifted with a dreadful beauty, almost spectral, that does not animate life, they march to their deaths, pale, insensible, superbly contemptuous, on the hearts they have crushed under their heels. From the departure of these amours, allied to hate, from pleasures more wounding than sorrow, the poet turns to his sad idol of exotic perfume, of savage attire, supple and wheedling as the black panther of Java, which remains always and compensates him for the spiteful Parisian cats with the pointed claws, playing with the heart of the poet as with a mouse. But it is to none of these creatures of plaster, marble, or ebony that he gives his soul. Above this black heap of leprous houses, this infectious labyrinth where the spectres of pleasure circle, this impure tingling of misery, of ugliness and perversity, far, far distant in the unalterable azure floats the adorable spirit of Beatrice, the ever-desired ideal, never attained; the supreme and divine beauty incarnated in the form of an ethereal woman, spiritualised, fashioned of light, fire, and perfume; a vapour, a dream, a reflection of the enchanted and seraphic world, like the

Sigeias, the Morellas, the Unas, the Leonores of Edgar Poe, and the Seraphita-Seraphitus of Balzac, that marvellous creation.

From the depths of his fall, his errors, and his despairs, it is towards this celestial image, as towards the Madonna of Bon-Secours, that he extends his arms with cries, tears, and a profound contempt for himself. In his hours of loving melancholy it is always with her he wishes to fly away and hide his perfect happiness in some mysterious fairy refuge, some cottage of Gainsborough, some home of Gerard Dow, or, better still, some marble palace of Benares or Hyderabad. Never did his dreams lead him into other company.

Can one see in this Beatrice, this Laura whom no name designates, a real young girl or woman, passionately loved by the poet during his life-time? It would be romantic to suppose so, but it has not been permitted to us to be intimate enough with the secret life of his soul to answer this question affirmatively or negatively.

In his metaphysical conversations, Baudelaire spoke much of his ideas, little of his sentiments, and never of his actions. As to the chapter of his loves, he for ever placed a seal upon his fine and disdainful lips. The safest plan would be to see in this ideal love a pleading only of the soul, the soaring of the unsatisfied heart, and the eternal sigh of the imperfect aspiring to the absolute.

At the end of the "Flowers of Evil" there is a set of poems on "Wine," and the different intoxications that it produces, according to the brain it attacks. It is unnecessary to say that they are not Bacchic songs celebrating the juice of the grape, or anything like it. They are hideous and terrible paintings of drunkenness, but without the morality of Hogarth. The picture has no need of a legend and the "Wine of the Workman" makes one shudder. The "Litanies of Satan," god of evil and prince of the world, are one of those cold, familiar ironies of the author, in which one would be wrong to see impiety. Impiety is not in the nature of Baudelaire, who believed in the superior law established by God for all eternity, the least infraction of which is punished by the severest chastisement, not only in this world, but in the future.

If he has painted vice and shown Satan in all his pomp, it is without the least complacence in the task. He also had a singular prepossession of the devil as a tempter in whom he saw a dragon who hurried him into sin, infamy, crime, and perversity. Fault in Baudelaire was always followed by remorse, contempt, anguish, despair; and the punishment was far worse than any corporal one could have been. But enough of this subject; we are critic, not theologian.

Let us point out, among the poems which comprise the "Flowers of Evil," some of the most remarkable; amongst others, that which is called, "Don Juan aux Enfers." It is a picture of tragic grandeur, painted in sombre and magisterial colours on the fiery vault of hell. The boat glides on the black waters, carrying Don Juan and his cortège of victims. The beggar whom he tried to make deny God, wretched athlete, proud in his rags like Antisthenes, paddles the oars to the domain of Charon. At the stern, a man of stone, a discoloured phantom, with rigid and sculptural gestures, holds the helm. The old Don Luis shows his whitened locks, scorned by his hypocritically impious son. Sganerelle demands the payment of his wages from his henceforth insolvent master. Donna Elvira tries to bring back the old smile of the lover to the disdainful lips of her husband; and the pale lovers, brought to evil, abandoned, betrayed, trampled under foot like flowers, expose the ever-open wounds of their hearts. Under this passion of tears, lamentations, and maledictions Don Juan remains unmoved; he has done what he has wished. Heaven, hell, and the world judge him, according to their understanding; his pride knows no remorse; the shot has been able to kill, but not to make him repent.

By its serene melancholy, its cheerful tranquillity, and oriental *kief* the poem entitled "La Vie Antérieure" contrasts happily with the sombre pictures of monstrous modern Paris, and shows that the artist has, on his palette, side by side with the blacks, bitumens, umbers, and siennas, a whole gamut of fresh tints: light, transparent, delicate roses, ideal blues, like the far-away Breughel of Paradise, with which to depict the Elysian Fields and mirage of his dreams.

It is well to note particularly the sentiment towards the *artificial* betrayed by the poet. By the word *artificial* one must understand a creation owing its existence entirely to Art, and from which Nature is entirely absent. In an article written during the life-time of Baudelaire, we pointed out this odd tendency of which to poem entitled "Rêve parisien" is a striking example. Here are the lines which endeavoured to lender this splendid and sombre nightmare, worthy of the engravings of Martynn: "Imagine a supernatural landscape, or rather a perspective in metal, marble, and water, from which all vegetation is banished. All is rigid, polished, mirrored under a sky without sun, without moon, without stars. In the midst of the silence of eternity rise up, artificially lit, palaces, colonnades, towers, stair-cases, fountains from which fall heavy cascades like curtains of crystal. The blue waters are encircled, like the steel of antique mirrors, in quays, basins of burnished gold, or run silently under bridges of precious stones. The crystallised ray enshrines the liquid, and the porphyry flagstones of the terraces reflect the surrounding objects like ice. The Queen of Sheba, walking there, would lift up her robe, fearing to wet her feet, so glistening is the surface. The style of this poem is brilliant, like black, polished marble."

Is it not a strange fantasy, this composition made from rigid elements, in which nothing lives, throbs, breathes, and where not a blade of grass, not a leaf, not a flower comes to derange the implacable symmetry of forms invented by Art? Does it not make one believe in the unblemished Palmyra or the Palenqué remaining standing on a dead planet bereft of its atmosphere?

These are, undoubtedly, strange imaginings, anti-natural, neighbours of hallucination and expressions of a secret desire for unattainable novelty; but, for our part, we prefer them to the insipid simplicity of the pretended poets who, on the threadbare canvas of the commonplace, embroider, with old wools faded in colour, designs of bourgeois triviality or of foolish sentimentality: crowns of roses, green leaves of cabbages, and doves pecking one another. Sometimes we do not fear to attain the rare at the expense of the shocking, the fantastic, and the exaggerated. Barbarity of language appeals to us more than platitude. Baudelaire has this advantage: he can be bad, but he is never common. His faults, like his good qualities, are original, and, even when he has displeased, he has, after long reasoning, willed it so.

Let us bring this analysis, already rather too long, however much we abridge it, to a close by a few words on that poem which so astonished Victor Hugo – "Petites Vieilles" The poet, walking in the streets of Paris, sees some little old women with humble and sad gait pass by. He follows them as one would pretty women, recognising from the threadbare cashmere, worn out, mended a hundred times, from the end of lace frayed and yellow, the ring – sorrowful souvenir, disputed by the pawn-broker and ready to leave the slender finger of the pale hand – a past of happier fortune and elegance: a life of love and devotion, perhaps; the remains of beauty under ruin and misery and the devastations of age. He reanimates all these trembling spectres, reclothes them, puts the flesh of youth on these emaciated skeletons, revives in these poor wounded hearts illusions of other days. Nothing could be more ridiculous, nothing more touching, than these Venuses of Père-Lachaise and these Ninons of Petits-Ménages who file off lamentably under the evocation of the master, like a procession of ghosts surprised by the day.

III

The question of versification and scansion, disdained by all those who have no appreciation of form – and they are numerous to-day – has been rightly judged by Baudelaire as one of the utmost importance. Nothing is more common now than to mistake technique in art for poetry itself. These are things which have no relation.

Fénelon, J. J. Rousseau, Bernardin de Saint Pierre, Chateaubriand, George Sand are poetic in principle, but not poets – that is to say, they are incapable of writing in verse, even mediocre verse, a special faculty often possessed by people of inferior merit to that of the great masters. To wish to separate technique from poetry is a modern folly which will lead to nothing but the annihilation of Art itself. We encountered, in an excellent article of Sainte-Beuve on Taine, à propos of Pope and Boileau, lightly treated by the author of "The History of English Literature" this clear and judicial paragraph, where things are brought to light by the great critic who was from the beginning, and is always, a great poet.

"But, à propos of Boileau, must I then accept this strange judgment of a man of *esprit*, this contemptuous opinion that M. Taine takes of him, and fear to endorse it in passing? – 'There are two sorts of verse in Boileau: the most numerous, which are those of a pupil of the third form of his school; the less numerous, which are those of a pupil of rhetoric.' The man of letters who speaks thus (Guillaume Guizot) does not feel that Boileau is a poet, and, I will go further, he ought not to be sensible of poetry in such a poet. I understand that one does not put all the poetry into the metre; but I cannot at all understand that, when the point in question is Art, one takes no account of Art itself, and depreciates the perfect workers who excel in it. Suppress with a single blow all the poetry in verse, or else speak with esteem of those who possess the secrets. Boileau was of the small number of those; Pope equally." One could not express it better nor more justly. When it is a question of a poet, the composition of his verse is a considerable thing and worthy of study, for it constitutes a great part of his intrinsic value. It is with this stamp his gold, his silver, his copper are coined.

The verse of Baudelaire is written according to modern methods and reform. The mobility of the cesura, the use of the *mot d'ordre*, the freedom of expression, the writing of a single Alexandrine, the clever mechanism of prosody, the turn of the stanza and the strophe – whatever its individual formula, its tabulated structure, its secrets of metre – bear the stamp of Baudelaire's sleight of hand, if one may express it thus. His signature, C. B., claims each rhyme he has made.

Among his poems there are many pieces which have the apparent disposition and exterior design of a sonnet, though "sonnet" is not written at the head of each of them. That undoubtedly comes from a literary scruple, and a prosodical conscience, the origin of which seems to us traceable to an article where he recounts his visit to us and relates our conversation. It must not be forgotten that he had just brought us a volume of verses of two absent friends, that he was commissioned to make known, and were lines in his narrative: "After having rapidly run through the volume, he remarked to me that the poets in question allowed themselves too often to write libertine sonnets, that is to say unorthodox, willingly breaking through the rule of the quadruple rhyme."

At this period the greater part of the "Flowers of Evil" was already composed, and in it there are to be found a large number of libertine sonnets, which not only have the quadruple rhyme, but in which also the rhymes are alternated in a quite irregular manner.

The young scholar always allows himself a number of libertine sonnets, and we avow it is particularly disagreeable to us. Why, if one wishes to be free and to arrange the rhyme according to individual fancy, choose a fixed form which admits of no digression, no caprice? The irregular in what should be regular, lack of form in what should be symmetrical – what can be more illogical and annoying? Each infraction of a rule disturbs us like a doubtful or a false note. The sonnet is a sort of poetical fugue in which the theme ought to pass and repass until its final resolution in a given form. One must be absolutely subservient to law, or else, if one finds these laws antiquated, pedantic, cramping, not write sonnets at all.

Baudelaire often sought musical effect by one or more particularly melodious lines recurring alternately, as in the Italian strophe called sextine, of which M. le Comte de Gramont offers in his poetry several happy examples. He applied this form, which has the vague, rocking sound of a magical incantation half heard in a dream, to the subjects of melancholy memory and unhappy loves. The stanzas, with their monotonous rustling, carry and express the thoughts, balancing them as the waves carry on their crests a drowning flower fallen from the shore.

Like Longfellow and Poe, Baudelaire sometimes employed alliteration; that is to say, the repetition of a certain consonant to produce in the interior of the verse a harmonious effect. Sainte-Beuve, to whom none of these delicate touches is unknown, and who continually practises them in his exquisite art, has once said in an Italian sonnet of deep gentleness: "Sorrente m'a rendu mon doux reve infini."

Any sensitive ear can understand the charm of this liquid sound four times repeated, and which seems to sweep one away to the infinity of a dream, like the wing of a gull in the surging blue of a Neapolitan sea. Alliteration is often to be found in the prose of Beaumarchais, and the Scandinavian poets make great use of it. These trifles will undoubtedly appear frivolous to utilitarians, progressive and practical men who think, with Stendhal, that verse is a childish form, good for primitive ages, and ask that poetry should be written in prose to suit a reasonable age. Yet all the same, these are details which make verse good or bad, and which make a man a poet or not.

Many-syllabled and full-sounding words pleased Baudelaire, and, with three or four of these, he often makes a line which seems immense, the sound of which is vibrant and prolongs the metre. For the poet, words have in themselves, and apart from the meanings they express, intrinsic beauty and value, like precious stones still uncut and not set in bracelets, in necklaces or in rings. They charm the connoisseur who watches and sorts them in the little chalice where they are put in reserve, as a goldsmith would his jewels. There are words of diamond, ruby, sapphire, emerald, and others which glisten phosphorescently when struck.

The great Alexandrines of which we have spoken, that come in times of lull and calm to die on the shore in the tranquillity and gentle undulation of the swelling surge, sometimes dash themselves to pieces in the foam and throw up their white spray against the sullen rocks, only to be tossed back immediately into the salt sea.

The lines of eight feet are brisk, strong, striking, like a cat-o'-nine-tails, lashing the shoulders of those who, with a wicked conscience, perform hypocritical actions. They also display strange caprices; the author encases in his metre, as in a frame of ebony, the nightly sights of a cemetery where the eyes of the owls shine in the shadows; and, behind the bronze-green curtains of the yew-trees, slide, with spectral steps, pick-pockets, devastators of tombs, thieves of the dead.

In these eight-feet lines he paints sinister skies where, above the gibbet, rolls a moon, grown sickly from the incantations of

Canidies. He describes the chill ennui of a dead person, who has exchanged his bed of luxury for the coffin, who dreams in his solitude, starting at each drop of icy rain that filters through his coffin-lid. He shows us, in his curiously disordered bouquet of faded flowers, old letters, ribbons, miniatures, pistols, daggers, and phials of laudanum. We see the room of the coward gallant where, in his absence, the ironical spectre of suicide comes, for Death itself cannot quench the fires of lust.

IV

From the composition of the verses let us pass to the style. Baudelaire intertwines his silken and golden threads with strong, rude hemp, as in a cloth worked by Orientals, at the same time gorgeous and coarse, where the most delicate ornamentations run in charming caprice on the fine camel's-hair, or on a cloth coarse to the touch like the sail of a boat. The most delicate, the most precious even, is hurled in with savage brutalities; and, from the scented boudoir and voluptuously languorous conversations, one falls into ignoble inns where drunkards, mixing blood with wine, dispute at the point of their knives for some Hélène from the streets.

"The Flowers of Evil" are the brightest gem in Baudelaire's crown. In them he has given play to his originality, and shown that one is able, after incalculable volumes of verse where every variety of subject seems to be exhausted, to bring to light something new and unexpected, without hauling down the sun and the stars, or making universal history file past as in a German fresco.

But what has especially made his name famous is his translation of Edgar Poe; for in France little is read of the poet except his prose, and it is the feuilletons that make the poems known. Baudelaire has almost naturalised for us this singular and rare individuality, so pregnant, so exceptional, who at first rather scandalised than charmed America. Not that his work is in any way morally shocking – he is, on the contrary, of virginal and seraphic chastity; but because he disturbed accepted principles and practical common sense, and, also, because there was no criterion by which to judge him.

Edgar Poe had none of the American ideas on progress, perfectibility, democratic institutions, and other subjects of declamation dear to the Philistines of the two worlds. He was not a worshipper of the god of gold; he loved poetry for itself and preferred beauty to utility – enormous heresy! Still, he had the good fortune to write well things that made the hair of fools in all countries stand on end. A grave director of a review or journal – a friend of Poe, moreover, and well-intentioned – avowed that it was difficult to employ him, and that one was obliged to pay him less than others, because he wrote above the heads of the vulgar – admirable reason!

The biographer of the author of the "Raven" and "Eureka," said that Edgar Poe, if he had regulated his genius and applied his creative powers in a way more appropriate to America, would have become a money-making author; but he was undisciplined, worked only when he liked, and on what subjects he pleased. His roving disposition made him roll like a comet out of its orbit from Baltimore to New York, from New York to Philadelphia, from Philadelphia to Boston or Richmond, without being able to settle anywhere. In his moments of ennui, distress, or breakdown, when to excessive excitement, caused by some feverish work, succeeded that despondency known to authors, he drank brandy, a fault for which he has been bitterly reproached by Americans, who, as every one knows, are models of temperance.

He was not under any delusion as to the effects of this disastrous vice, he who has written in the "Black Cat" this prophetic phrase: "What illness is comparable to alcohol!" He drank without drunkenness, just to forget, to find himself in a happy mood in regard to his work, or even to end an intolerable life in evading the scandal of a direct suicide. Briefly, one day, seized in the street by an attack of delirium tremens, he was carried to the hospital where he died, still young and with no signs of decaying power. The deplorable habit had had no influence on his intellect or his manners, which remained always those of an accomplished gentleman; nor on his beauty, which was remarkable to the end.

We indicate but rapidly some traits of Edgar Poe, as we are not writing his life. The American author held so high a place in the intellectual esteem of Baudelaire that we must speak of him in a more or less developed way, and give, if not an account of his life, at least of his doctrines. Edgar Poe has certainly influenced Baudelaire, his translator, especially during the latter part of his life, which was, alas! so short.

"The Extraordinary Histories," "The Narrative of Arthur Gordon Pym," "The Tales of the Grotesque and Arabesque," "Eureka," have been translated by Baudelaire with so exact a correspondence in style and thought, a freedom so faithful yet so supple, that the translations produce the effect of original work, and are almost perfect. "The Extraordinary Histories" are preceded by a piece of high criticism, in which the translator analyses the eccentric and novel talent of Poe, which France, with her utter heedlessness of the originalities of foreigners, ignored profoundly till Baudelaire revealed them. He brought to bear upon this work, necessary to explain a nature so beyond the vulgar idea, a metaphysical sagacity of the rarest delicacy. The pages may be counted the most remarkable he has ever written.

Great excitement was created by these histories, so mathematically fantastic, deduced in algebraical formulæ, and in which the expositions resemble some judiciary led by the most subtle and perspicacious magistrates.

"The Murders in the Rue Morgue," "The Purloined Letter," "The Gold-Bug," enigmas more difficult to divine than those of the Sphinx, and in which the interest, sustained to the very end, excites to delirium the public, surfeited with romances and adventures. One feels deeply for Auguste Dupin, with his strange, divinatory lucidity, who seems to hold between his hands the threads, drawing one to the other, of thoughts most opposed, and who arrives at his conclusions by deductions of a marvellous correctness. One admires Legrand, cleverer still at deciphering cryptograms than Claude Jacquet, employed by the Ministry, who read to Desmarets, in the history of the "13," the letter deciphered by Ferrango; and the result of this reading is the discovery of the treasures of Captain Kidd! Every one will confess that he would have had to be very clear-sighted to trace in the glimmer of the flame, in the red characters on yellow parchment, the death's-head, the kid, the lines and points, the cross, the tree and its branches, and to guess where the corsair had buried the coffer full of diamonds, jewels, watches, golden chains, ounces, doubloons, dollars, piastres, and money from all countries, the discovery of which recompensed the sagacity of Legrand. The "Pit and the Pendulum" caused terror equal to the blackest inventions of Anne Radcliffe, of Lewis, and of the Rev. Father Mathurin, while one gets giddy watching the tearing whirlpool of the Maelstrom, colossal, funnel-like walls upon which ships run like pieces of straw in a tempest.

"The Truth of the Case of M. Waldemar," shakes the nerves even of the most robust, and the "Fall of the House of Usher" inspires profound melancholy.

Imaginative natures were deeply touched by the faces of women, so vaporous, transparent, romantically pale, and of almost spiritual beauty, that the poet named Morelia, Ligeia, Lady Rowena, Trevanion, de Tremaine, Lenore; but who are in reality only the incarnations under different forms of a unique love surviving the death of the adored one.

Henceforth, in France, the name of Baudelaire is inseparable from that of Edgar Poe, and the memory of the one immediately awakes thoughts of the other. It seems sometimes that the ideas of the American were really of French origin.

Baudelaire, like the greater number of the poets of his time, when the Arts, less separated than they were formerly, mingled more one with another and allowed of frequent transposition, had the taste for, sentiment and knowledge of, painting. He wrote noteworthy articles in the "Salon," and, amongst others, pamphlets on Delacroix, which analysed with clear penetration and subtlety the nature of a great romantic painter. He thought deeply, and we find, in some reflections on Edgar Poe, this significant phrase: "Like our Delacroix, who has raised his art to the height of great poetry, Edgar Poe likes to place his subjects on violet and green backgrounds which reveal the phosphorescence and the fragrance of the storm." How just is this sentiment, so simply phrased, incidental to the passionate and feverish colour of the painter! Delacroix, in effect, charmed Baudelaire by the "maladie" even of his talent, so troubled, restless, nervous, excitable, and so tormented with uneasiness, melancholy, febrile ardour, convulsive efforts, and the vague dreams of modern times.

At one time, the realistic school believed it could monopolise Baudelaire. Certain outrageously crude and truthful pictures in the "Flowers of Evil," pictures in which the poet had not hesitated before any ugliness, might have made some superficial minds think he leaned towards that doctrine. They did not note that these pictures, so-called real, were always ennobled by character, effect, or colour, and also served as a contrast to the smooth and idealistic work. Baudelaire, allowing himself to be drawn by these realists, visited their studios and was to have written an article on Courbet, the painting-master of Ornans, which, however, never appeared. Nevertheless, to one of the later Salons, Fantin, in the odd frame where he united round the medallion of Eugène Delacroix, like the supernumeraries of an apotheosis, the painters, and writers known as realists, placed Baudelaire in a corner of it with his serious look and ironical smile. Certainly Baudelaire, as an admirer of Delacroix, had a right to be there. But did he intellectually and sympathetically make a part of this company, whose tendencies were not in accord with his aristocratic tastes and aspirations towards the beautiful? In him, as we have already said, the employment of trivial and natural ugliness was only a sort of manifestation and protestation of horror; and we doubt if the Venus de Courbet had ever much charm for him, the amateur of exquisite elegance, refined mannerisms, and mannered evasions. Not that he was incapable of admiring grandiose beauty; he who has written "La Géante" ought to love "The Night" and the "Dawn," those magnificent colossal females that Michelangelo has placed on the voluta of the tombs of the Medici. Baudelaire had, moreover, metaphysical and philosophical tenets which could not but alienate him from this school, to which he had no pretext for attaching himself.

Far from being satisfied with reality, he sought diligently for the bizarre, and, if he met with some singular, original type, he followed it, studied it, and learnt how to find the end of the thread on the bobbin and so to unravel it. Thus he was familiar with Guys, a mysterious individual, who occupied his time in going to all the odd corners of the universe where anything was taking place to obtain sketches for English illustrated journals.

This Guys, whom we knew, was at one time a great traveller, a profound and quick observer, and a perfect humorist. In the flash of an eye he seized upon the characteristic side of men and things; in a few strokes of the pencil he silhouetted them in his album, tracing the cursive lines with the pen like a stenographer, and washing them over with a flat tint to indicate the colour.

Guys was not what is properly called an artist, but he had the particular gift of sketching the chief points of things rapidly. In a flash of the eye, with an unequalled clear-sightedness, he disentangled from all the traits – just the one. He placed it in prominence, instinctively or designedly, rejecting the merely complementary parts.

No one was more reproachful than he of a pose, a "cassure," to use a vulgar word which exactly expresses our thought, whether in a dandy or in a *voyou*, in a great lady or in a daughter of the people. He possessed in a rare degree the sense of modern corruptions, in high as in low society, and he also culled, under the form of sketches, his flowers of evil. No one could render like Guys the elegant slenderness and sleekness of the race-horse, the dainty border on the skirt of a little lady drawn by her ponies, the pose of the powdered and befurred coachman on the box of a great chariot, with panels emblazoned with the coat of arms, going to a "drawing-room" accompanied by three footmen. He seems, in this style of drawing, fashionable and cursive, consecrated to the scenes of high life, to have been the precursor of the intelligent artists of "La Vie Parisienne," Marcelin, Hadol, Morin, Crafty. But, if Guys expressed, according to the principles of Brummel, dandyism and the allurements of the *duckery*, he excelled no less in portraying the venal nymphs of Piccadilly and the Argyle Rooms with their flash toilets and bold eyes. He was not afraid to occupy himself with the deserted lanes, and to sketch there, under the light of the moon or in the flickering glimmer of a gas-jet, a silhouette of one of the spectres of pleasure who haunt the streets of London. If he found himself in Paris, he followed the extreme fashions of the wicked place and what is known as the "coqueterie du ruisseau." You can imagine that Guys sought there only "character." It was his passion, and he separated with astonishing certainty the picturesque and singular side of the types from the allurements and costume of the time. Talent of this kind could not but charm Baudelaire, who, in effect, greatly esteemed Guys. We possessed about sixty drawings, sketches, aquarelles of this humorist, and we gave some of them to the poet. The present gave him great pleasure, and he carried it joyfully away.

Certainly he realised all that was lacking in these rough sketches, to which Guys himself attached not the slightest importance once they had been traced on wood by the clever engravers of the "Illustrated London News." But Baudelaire was struck by the spirit, the clear-sightedness, and powerful observation they displayed, literary qualities graphically translated in the language of line. He loved in these drawings the complete absence of antiquity – that is to say, of classical tradition – and the deep sentiment of what we call "decadence," for lack of a word more expressive of our meaning. But we know what Baudelaire understood by "decadence." Did he not say somewhere, à propos of these literary distinctions: – "It seems to me that two women are presented to me; the one a rustic matron, rude in health and virtue, without allurement or worth; briefly, *owing nothing except to simple nature*; the other, one of those beauties who dominate and fascinate the mind, uniting, with her powerful and original charm, all the eloquence of the toilet, mistress of her bearing, conscious and queen of herself, with a voice of harmonious melody, and dreamy gaze allowed to travel whither it will. My choice cannot be doubted, however many pedagogues reproach me with lack of classical honour?"

This so original comprehension of modern beauty turns the question, for it regards antique beauty as primitive, coarse, barbarous; a paradoxical opinion undoubtedly, but one which can be upheld. Balzac much preferred, to the Venus of Milo, a Parisienne *élégante*, delicate, coquettish, draped in cashmere, going furtively on foot to some rendezvous, her chantilly violet held to her nose, her head bent in such a way as to display, between the brim of her hat and the last fold of her shawl, the nape of a neck like a column of ivory, over which some stray curl glistens in the sunlight. This has its charms; but, for our part, we prefer the Venus of Milo.

With such ideas as these one can imagine that for some time Baudelaire was inclined towards the realistic school of which Courbet is the god and Manet the high-priest. But if certain sides of his nature were such as could be satisfied by direct, and not traditional, representation of ugliness, or at least of contemporary triviality, his aspirations for Art, elegance, luxury, and beauty led him towards a superior sphere. And Delacroix, with his febrile passion, his stormy colours, his poetical melancholy, his palette of the setting sun, and his clever expression of the decadence, was, and remained, his master by election.

We come now to a singular work of Baudelaire's, half

translation, half original, entitled, "The artificial Paradises, Opium and Hashish," and at which we must pause; for it has contributed not a little to the idea among the public, who are always happy in spreading unfavourable reports of authors, that the writer of the "Flowers of Evil" was in the habit of seeking inspiration in these stimulants. His death, following upon a stroke of paralysis which made him powerless to express the thoughts in his brain, only confirmed this belief. This paralysis, so it was said, came undoubtedly from excess in hashish or opium, to which the poet first gave himself up out of love of peculiarity, and then from that fatal craving these drugs produce.

His illness was caused by nothing but the fatigue, ennui, sorrow, and embarrassments inherent in literary people whose talent does not admit of regular work, easy to sell, like journalism, and whose works, by their originality, frighten the timid directors of reviews. Baudelaire was as sober as all other workers, and, while admitting a taste for the creation of an "artificial paradise," by means of some stimulant, opium, hashish, wine, alcohol, or tobacco, seems to follow the nature of man – since one finds it in all periods, in all conditions, in all countries, barbarous or civilised – he saw in it the proof of original perversity, a means of escaping *necessary* sorrow, a satanical suggestion for usurping, even in the present, the happiness reserved as a recompense for resignation, virtue, and the persistent effort towards the good and the beautiful. He thought that the devil said to the eaters of hashish, the smokers of opium, as in the olden times to our first parents, "If you taste of the fruit you will be as the gods," and that he no more kept his word than he did to Adam and Eve; for, the next day, the god, tempted, weakened, enervated, descended lower than the beast and remained isolated in an immense space, having no other resource to escape himself than by recourse to his poison, the doses of which he gradually increases. That he once or twice tried hashish, as a psychological experience, is possible and even probable; but he did not make continuous use of it. This happiness, bought at the chemist's and carried in the pocket, was repugnant to him, and he compared the ecstasy that it produced to that of a maniac, for whom painted cloth and coarse decorations replaced real furniture and the garden enriched with living flowers. He came but rarely, and then only as a spectator, to the séances at the Hôtel Pimodan, where our circle met to take the "dawamesk"; séances that we have already described in the "Review of the Two Worlds," under this title: "The Club of the Hashishins." After some ten experiments we renounced once and for all this intoxicating drug, not only because it made us ill physically, but also because the true littérateur has need only of natural dreams, and he does not wish his thoughts to be influenced by any outside agency.

Balzac came to one of these soirées, and Baudelaire related his visit thus: "Balzac undoubtedly thought that there is no greater shame or keener suffering than the abdication of the will. I saw him once at a reunion when he was contemplating the prodigious effects of hashish. He listened and questioned with attention and amusing vivacity. People who knew him would guess that he was bound to be interested. The idea shocked him in spite of himself. Some one presented him with the dawamesk. He examined it, smelt it, and gave it back without touching it. The struggle between his almost infantile curiosity and his repugnance for the abdication, betrayed itself in his expressive face; love of dignity prevailed. In effect, it is difficult to imagine the theorist of 'will' the spiritual twin of Louis Lambert, consenting to lose even a particle of this precious *substance*."

We were at the Hôtel Pimodan that evening, and therefore can relate this little anecdote with perfect accuracy. Only, we would add this characteristic detail: in giving back the spoonful of hashish that was offered him, Balzac only said that the attempt would be useless, and that hashish, he was sure, would have no action on his brain. That was possible. This powerful brain, in which *will power* was enthroned and fortified by study, saturated with the subtle aroma of moka, and never obscured by even a few bottles of the lightest of wine of Vouvray, would perhaps have been capable of resisting the passing intoxication of Indian hemp. For hashish, or dawamesk, we have forgotten to say, is only a concoction of *cannabis indica*, mixed to a fleshy substance with honey and pistachio-nuts, to give it the consistence of a paste or preserve.

The analysis of hashish is medically very well done in the "Artificial Paradises," and science is able to cull from them certain information; for Baudelaire prided himself on his accuracy, and on no consideration whatever would he slur over the least technical ornamentation of this habit in which he had himself indulged. He specifies perfectly the real character of the hallucinations produced by hashish, which of itself creates nothing, simply developing the particular disposition of the individual, exaggerating it to the very last degree. What one sees is oneself, aggrandised, made sensitive, excited, immoderately outside time and space, at one time real but soon deformed, accentuated, enlarged, and in which each detail, with extreme intensity, becomes of supernatural importance. Yet all this is easily understandable to the hashish-eater, who divines the mysterious correspondence between the often incongruous images. If you hear a piece of music which seems as though performed by some celestial orchestra and a choir of seraphim, compared to which the symphonies of Haydn, of Mozart, and of Beethoven are no more than aggravating clatter, you may believe that it is only that a hand has skimmed over the keys of a piano in some vague prelude, or that a distant organ murmurs through the uproar of the streets – a well-known piece from the opera. If your eyes are dazzled by blinding lights, scintillations, and flames, assuredly it is only a certain number of candles that burn in the torches and flambeaux.

As to the walls, ceasing to be opaque, sinking away into vaporous perspective, deep, blue, like a window opening on the infinite, it is but a glass mirror opposite the dreamer with its mingled and transparently fantastic shadows. The nymphs, the goddesses, the gracious apparitions, burlesque or terrible, come out of the pictures, the tapestries, from the statues displaying their mythological nudity in the niches, or from the grimacing china figures on the shelves.

It is the same with the olfactory ecstasies which transport one to the paradises of perfumes, of marvellous flowers, balancing their calices like censors which send out aromatic scents of penetrating subtlety, recalling the memory of former lives, of balsamic and distant shores and primitive loves in some Tahiti of a dream. One does not have to seek far in the room for a pot of heliotrope or tuberose, a sachet of Spanish leather or a cashmere shawl impregnated with patchouli, negligently thrown over the arm of a chair.

It is understood, then, if one wishes to enjoy to the full the magic of hashish, it is necessary to prepare in advance and furnish in some way the *motif* to its extravagant variations and disorderly fantasies. It is important to be in a tranquil frame of mind and body, to have on this day neither anxiety, duty, nor fixed time, and to find oneself in such an apartment as Baudelaire and Edgar Poe loved, a room furnished with poetical comfort, bizarre luxury, and mysterious elegance; a private and hidden retreat which seems to await the beloved, the ideal feminine face that Chateaubriand, in his noble language, calls the "sylphide." In such circumstances, it is probable, and even almost certain, that the naturally agreeable sensations turn into ravishing blessings, ecstasies, ineffable pleasure, much superior to the coarse joys promised to the faithful in the paradise of Mahomet, too easily comparable to a seraglio. The green, red, and white houris coming out from the hollow pearl that they inhabit and offering themselves to the faithful, would appear as vulgar women compared to the nymphs, angels, sylphides, perfumed vapours, ideal transparencies, forms of blue and rose let loose on the disc of the sun and coming from the depths of infinity with stellary transports, like the silver globules on gaseous liquor, from the bottom of the crystal chalice, that the hashish-eater sees in innumerable legions in the dreams he dreams while wide-awake.

Without these precautions the ecstasy is likely to turn into-nightmare. Pleasure changes to suffering, joy to terror; a terrible anguish seizes one by the heart and breaks one with its fantastically enormous weight, as though the sphinx of the pyramids, or the elephant of the king of Siam, had amused itself by flattening one out. At other times an icy cold is felt making the victim seem like marble up to the hips, like the king in the "Thousand and One Nights," half changed to a statue, whose wicked wife came every morning to beat the still supple shoulders.

Baudelaire relates two or three hallucinations of men of different temperaments, and one experienced by a woman in a small room hidden by a gilt trellis and festooned with flowers, which is easily recognised as the boudoir of the Hôtel Pimodan. He accompanies each vision with an analytical and moral commentary, through which his unconquerable repugnance for happiness obtained by such means is easily discernible. He counts as nothing the consideration of the help that genius can draw from the ideas suggested by intoxication of hashish. Firstly, these ideas are not so beautiful as one imagines, their charm comes chiefly from the extreme excitement in which the subject is. Then hashish, which produces these ideas, destroys at the same time the power of using them, for it reduces to nothing the will and plunges its victims in an cnnui in which the mind becomes incapable of any effort or work, and from which it cannot escape except through the medium of another dose. "Lastly," he adds, "admitting the minute hypothesis of a temperament well enough balanced, strong enough to resist the evil effects of this perfidious drug, it is necessary to consider another fatal, terrible danger, which is that of habit. Those who have recourse to a poison to make them think, will soon find that they cannot think without poison. Picture to yourself the terrible fate of a man whose paralysed imagination no longer fulfils its functions without the aid of hashish or opium."

And, a little later, he makes his profession of faith in these noble terms: "But man is not so lacking in honest means of inspiration that he is obliged to invite the aid of the pharmacy or of sorcery; he has no need to sell his soul to pay for the intoxicating caresses and friendliness of the houris. What is the paradise that one buys at the price of eternal salvation?"

There follows the painting of a sort of Olympus placed on the arduous mount of spirituality where the muses of Raphael or of Mantegna, under the guidance of Apollo, surround with their rhythmical choirs the artist vowed to the cult of beauty and recompense him for his continuous efforts. "Beneath him," continues the author, "at the foot of the mountain, in the brambles and mud, the troop of men, the band of helots, simulate the grimaces of enjoyment, and yell out if the bite of poison is taken away from them; and the saddened poet says: 'These unfortunate beings who have neither fasted nor prayed, and who have refused to work out their own redemption, demand from black magic the means of elevation, with a sudden stroke, to a supernatural existence. Magic dupes them and kindles in them false happiness and light; whilst we, poets and philosophers, who have given new life to our souls by continued work and thought, by the assiduous exercise of the will and permanent nobility of intention, we have created for our pleasure a garden of real beauty. Confiding in the word which says faith can remove mountains, we have accomplished the only miracle which God has allowed.'"

After such an expression of faith it is difficult to believe that the author of the "Flowers of Evil," in spite of his satanical leanings, has often visited artificial paradises.

Succeeding the study on hashish is one on the subject of opium. But here Baudelaire had for his guidance a book, singularly celebrated in England, "Confessions of an English Opium Eater," by De Quincey, a distinguished Hellenist, a leading writer, and a man of great respectability, who has dared, with tragical candour, in a country the most hardened by cant in the world, to avow his passion for opium, to describe this passion, representing the phases, the intermittences, the relapses, the combats, the enthusiasms, the prostrations, the ecstasies and the phantasmagoria followed by inexpressible anguish. De Quincey, incredible as it may seem, had, augmenting little by little each dose, come to taking eight thousand drops a day. This, however, did not prevent him from living till the age of seventy-five, for he only died in the month of December 1859, making the doctors, to whom, in a fit of *humour*, he had mockingly left his corpse as a subject for scientific experiment, wait a long time. This habit did not prevent him from publishing a crowd of literary and learned works in which nothing announced the fatal influence which he himself described as "the black idol." The *dénouement* of the book leaves it understood that only with superhuman efforts was the author brought to the state of self-correction; but that could only have been a sacrifice to morals and conventions, like the recompense of virtue and the punishment of crime at the end of a melodrama, final impenitence being a bad example. And De Quincey pretends that, after seventeen years of use and eight years of abuse of opium, he has been able to renounce this dangerous substance! It is unnecessary to discourage the *theriakis* of good-will. But what of the love, however expressed, in the lyrical invocation to the brown liqueur?

"O just, subtle, and all-conquering opium! thou who, to the hearts of rich and poor alike, for the wounds that will never heal, and for the pangs of grief that 'tempt the spirit to rebel' bringest an assuaging balm; – eloquent opium! that with thy potent rhetoric stealest away the purposes of wrath, pleadest effectually for relenting pity, and through one night's heavenly sleep callest back to the guilty man the visions of his infancy, and hands washed pure from blood; – O just and righteous opium! that to the chancery of dreams summonest, for the triumphs of despairing innocence, false witnesses; and confoundest perjury; and dost reverse the sentences of unrighteous judges; – thou buildest upon the bosom of darkness, out of the fantastic imagery of the brain, cities and temples, beyond the art of Phidias and Praxiteles – beyond the splendours of Babylon and Hekatompylos; and, 'from the anarchy of dreaming sleep,' callest into sunny light the faces of long-buried beauties, and the blessed household countenances, cleansed from the 'dishonours of the grave.' Thou only givest these gifts to man; and thou hast the keys of Paradise, O just, subtle, and mighty opium!"

Baudelaire does not translate De Quincey's book entirely. He takes from it the most salient parts, of which he writes in an analysis intermingled with digressions and philosophical reflections, in such a way that he presents the entire work in an abridgment. Nothing is more curious than the biographical details which open these confessions. They show the flight of the scholar to escape from the tyrannies of his tutors, his miserable and starving life in the great desert of London, his sojourn in the lodgings turned into a garret by the negligence of the proprietor. We read of his liaison with a little half-idiot servant, Ann, a poor child, sad violet of the highways, innocent and virginal so far; his return in grace to his family and his becoming possessed of a fortune, considerable enough to allow him to give himself up entirely to his favourite studies in a charming cottage, in company with a noble woman, whom this Orestes of opium called his Electra. For, after his neuralgic pains, he had got into that ineradicable habit of taking the poison of which he absorbed, without disastrous results, the enormous quantity of forty grains a day.

To the most striking visions which shone with the blue and silver of Paradise or Elysium succeeded others more sombre than Erebus, to which one can apply the frightful lines of the poet:

"As when some great painter dips
His pen in gloom of earthquake and eclipse."

De Quincey, who was a precocious and distinguished humanist – he knew both Greek and Latin at the age of ten – had always taken great pleasure in reading Livy, and the words "Consul Romanus" resounded in his ears like a magical and peremptorily irresistible formula. These five syllables struck upon his ear like the blasts of trumpets, sounding triumphal fanfares, and when, in his dreams, multitudes of enemies struggled on a field of battle lighted with livid glimmerings, with the rattling of guns and heavy tramping, like the surge of distant waters, suddenly a mysterious voice would cry out these dominating words: "Consul Romanus." A great silence would fall, oppressed by anxious waiting, and the consul would appear mounted on a white horse, in the midst of a great crowd, like the Marius of the "Batailles des Cimbres" of Decamps, and, with a fatidical gesture, decide the victory.

At other times, people seen in reality would be mixed up in his dreams, and would haunt them like obstinate spectres not to be chased away by any formula of exorcism.

One day, in the year 1813, a Malay, of a yellow and bilious colour, with sad, home-sick eyes, coming from London and seeking some haven, knowing not one word of any European language, knocked to see if he could rest a while, at the door of the cottage. Not wishing to fall short in the eyes of his domestics and neighbours, De Quincey spoke to him in Greek; the Asiatic replied in Malay, and his honour as a linguist was saved. After having given him some money, the master of the cottage, moved by the charity which causes a smoker to offer a cigar to a poor devil whom he supposes has long been without tobacco, gave the Malay a large piece of opium, which the man swallowed in a mouthful. There was enough to kill seven or eight unaccustomed people, but the yellow-skinned man was in the habit of taking it, for he went away with signs of great satisfaction and gratitude. He was not seen again, at least in the flesh, but he became one of the most assiduous frequenters of De Quincey's visions. The Malay of the saffron face and the strangely black eyes was a kind of genus of the extreme Orient who had the keys of India, Japan, China, and other countries of repute in a chimerical and impossible distance. As one obeys a guide whom one has not called, but whom one must follow by one of those fatalities that a dream admits of, De Quincey, in the steps of the Malay, plunged into regions of fabulous antiquity and inexpressible strangeness that caused him the profoundest terror. "I know not," says he in his "Confessions," "if others share my feelings on this point; but I have often thought that, if I were compelled to forgo England, and to live in China, among Chinese manners and methods and scenery, I should go mad.... A young Chinese seems to me an antediluvian man renewed. ... In China, over and above what it has in common with the rest of Southern Asia, I am terrified by the modes of life, by the manners, by the barrier of utter abhorrence placed between myself and *them*, by counter-sympathies deeper than I can analyse. I could sooner live with lunatics, with vermin, with crocodiles or snakes."

With malicious irony, the Malay, who seemed to understand the repugnance of the opium-eater, took care to lead him to the centre of great towns, to the ivory towers, to rivers full of junks crossed by bridges in the form of dragons, to streets encumbered with an innumerable population of baboons, lifting their heads with obliquely set eyes, and moving their tails like rats, murmuring, with forced reverence, complimentary mono-syllables.

The third and last part of the dreams of an opium-eater has a lamentable title, which, however, is well justified, "Suspiria de profundis." In one of these visions appeared three unforgettable figures, mysteriously terrible like the Grecian "Moires" and the "Mothers" of the second "Faust." These are the followers of Levana, the austere goddess who takes up the new-born babe and perfects it by sorrow. As there were three Graces, three Fates, three Furies, three Muses in the primitive ages, so there were three goddesses of sorrow; they are our Notre-Dame des Tristesses. The eldest of the three sisters is called Mater lacrymarum, or Our Lady of Tears; the second Mater suspiriorum, Our Lady of Sighs; the third and youngest, Mater tenebrarum, Our Lady of Darkness, the most redoubtable of all, and of whom the strongest cannot dream without a secret terror. These mournful spectres do not speak the language of mortals; they weep, they sigh, and make terrible gestures in the shadows. Thus they express their unknown sorrows, their nameless anguish, the suggestions of solitary despair, all that there is of suffering, bitterness, and sorrow in the depths of the human soul. Man ought to take warning from these initiators: "Thus will he see things that ought not to be seen, sights which are abominable, and unspeakable secrets; thus will he read the ancient truths, the sad, great, and terrible truths."

One can imagine that Baudelaire did not spare De Quincey the reproaches he addressed to all those who sought to attain the supernatural by material means; but, in regard to the beauty of the pictures painted by the illustrious and poetical dreamer, he showed him great good will and admiration.

About this time Baudelaire left Paris and pitched his tent in Brussels. One must not presume that this journey was taken with any political idea, but merely from the desire of a more tranquil and reposeful life, far away from the distractions and excitements of Paris. This change does not appear to have been a particularly profitable one for him. He worked little at Brussels, and his papers contain only sketchy notes, summaries almost hieroglyphical, which he alone could resolve. His health, instead of improving, was impaired, more deeply than he himself was aware, as the climate did not agree with him. The first symptoms manifested themselves in a certain slowness of speech, and a more and more marked hesitation in the choice of his words; but, as Baudelaire often expressed himself in a solemn and sententious way, one did not take much notice of this embarrassment in speech, which was the preface to the terrible malady that carried him off.

The rumour of Baudelaire's death spread in Paris with the winged rapidity of bad news, faster than an electric current along its wire. Baudelaire was still living, but the news, though false, was only premature; he could not recover from the attack. Brought back from Brussels by his family and friends, he lived some months, unable to speak, unable to write, as paralysis had broken the connecting thread between thought and speech. *Thought* lived in him always – one could see that from the expression of his eyes; but it was a prisoner, and dumb, without any means of communication, in the dungeon of clay which would only open in the tomb. What good is it to go into the details of this sad end? It is not a happy way to die; it is sorrowful, for the survivors, to see so fine and fruitful an intelligence pass away, to lose in a more and more deserted path of life a companion of youth.

Besides the "Flowers of Evil," translations of Edgar Poe, the "Artificial Paradises," and art criticisms, Baudelaire left a little book of "poems in prose" inserted at various periods in journals and reviews, which soon became without interest for vulgar readers and forced the poet, in his noble obstinacy, which would allow of no concession, to take the series to a more enterprising or literary paper. This is the first time that these pieces, scattered and difficult to find, are bound in one volume, nor will they be the least of the poet's titles to the regard of posterity.

In the short Preface addressed to Arsène Houssaye, which precedes the "Petits poèmes en prose," Baudelaire relates how the idea of employing this hybrid form, floating between verse and prose, came to him.

"I have a little confession to make to you. It was in turning over, for the twentieth time, the famous 'Gaspard de la nuit' of Aloysius Bertrand (a book known to me, to you, and several of our friends – has it not the right to be called famous?) that the idea came to me to attempt something analogous and to apply to the description of modern life, or rather to a modern and more abstract life, the process that he has applied to the painting of an ancient time, so strangely picturesque.

"Who among us, in these days of ambition, has not dreamt of the miracle of poetical, musical prose, without rhythm, without rhyme, supple enough and apt enough to adapt itself to the movements of the soul, to the swaying of a dream, to the sudden throbs of conscience?"

It is unnecessary to say that nothing resembles "Gaspard de la nuit" less than the "Poems in Prose." Baudelaire himself saw this after he commenced work, and he spoke of an *accident*, of which any other than he would have been proud, but which only humiliated a mind which looked upon the accomplishment of *exactly* what it had intended as an honour.

We have seen that Baudelaire always claimed to direct his inspiration according to his own will, and to introduce infallible mathematics into his art. He blamed himself for producing anything but that upon which he had resolved, even though it is, as in the present case, an original and powerful work.

Our poetical language, it must be acknowledged, in spite of the valiant effort of the new school to render it flexible and malleable, hardly lends itself to rare and subtle detail, especially when the subject is *la vie moderne*, familiar or luxurious. Without having, as at one time, a horror for the calculated word and a love of circumlocution, French verse, by its very construction, refuses particularly significant expressions and if forced into direct statement, immediately becomes hard, rugged, and laborious. "The Poems in Prose" came very opportunely to supply this deficiency, and in this form, which demands perfect art and where each word must be thrown, before being employed, into scales more easy to weigh down than those of the "Peseurs d'or" of Quintin Metsys – for it is necessary to have the standard, the weights, and the balance – Baudelaire has shown a precious side of his delicate and bizarre talent. He has been able to approach the almost inexpressible and to render the fugitive nuances which float between sound and colour, and those thoughts which resemble arabesque *motifs* or themes of musical phrases. It is not only to the physical nature, but to the secret movements of the soul, to capricious melancholy, to nervous hallucinations that this form is aptly applied. The author of the "Flowers of Evil" has drawn from it marvellous effects, and one is sometimes surprised that the language carries one through the transparencies of a dream, in the blue distances, marks out a ruined tower, a clump of trees, the summit of a mountain, and shows one things impossible to describe, which, until now, have never been expressed in words. This should be one of the glories, if not the greatest, of Baudelaire, to bring within the range of style a series of things, sensations, and effects unnamed by Adam, the great nomenclator. A writer can be ambitious of no more beautiful title, and this the author of the "Poems in prose" undoubtedly merits.

It is very difficult, without writing at great length – and, even then, it is better to direct the reader straight to the poems themselves – to give a just idea of these compositions; pictures, medallions, bas-reliefs, statuettes, enamels, pastels, cameos which follow each other rather like the vertebrae in the spine of a serpent. One is able to pick out some of the rings, and the pieces join themselves together, always living, having each its own soul writhing convulsively towards an inaccessible ideal.

Before closing this Introduction, which, although already too long – for we have simply chased through the work of the author and friend whose talent we endeavour to explain – it is necessary to quote the titles of the "Poems in Prose" – very superior in intensity, concentration, profoundness, and elegance to the delicate fantasies of "Gaspard de la nuit," which Baudelaire proposed to take as models. Among the fifty pieces which comprise the collection, each different in tone and composition, we will number "Le Gâteau, "La Chambre double," "Le Foules," "Les Veuves," "Le vieux saltimbanque," "Une Hémisphère dans une chevelure," "L'Invitation au voyage," "La Belle Dorothée," "Une Mort héroïque," "Le Thyrse," Portraits de maîtresses," "Le Désir de peindre," "Un Cheval de race" and especially "Les Bienfaits de la lune," an adorable poem in which the poet expresses, with magical illumination, what the English painter Millais has missed so completely in his "Eve of St. Agnes" – the descent of the nocturnal star with its phosphoric blue light, its grey of iridescent mother-of-pearl, its mist traversed by rays in which atoms of silver beat like moths. From the top of her stairway of clouds, the Moon leans down over the cradle of a sleeping child, bathing it in her baneful and splendid light; she dowers the sweet pale head like a fairy god-mother, and murmurs in its ear: "Thou shalt submit eternally to the influence of my kiss, thou shalt be beautiful after my fashion. Thou shalt love what I love and those that love me: the waters, the clouds, the silence, the night, the great green sea, the shapeless and multiform waters, the place where thou art not, the lover whom thou knowest not, the prodigious flowers, the perfumes that trouble the mind, the cats which swoon and groan like women in hoarse or gentle voices."

We know of no other analogy to this perfect piece than the poetry of Li-tai-pe, so well translated by Judith Walter, in which the Empress of China draws, among the rays, on the stairway of jade made brilliant by the moon, the folds of her white satin robe. A *lunatique* only is able to understand the moon and her mysterious charm.

When we listen to the music of Weber we experience at first a sensation of magnetic sleep, a sort of appeasement which separates us without any shock from real life. Then in the distance sounds a strange note which makes us listen attentively. This note is like a sigh from the supernatural world, like the voice of the invisible spirits which call us. Oberon just puts his hunting-horn to his mouth and the magic forest opens, stretching out into blue vistas peopled with all the fantastic folk described by Shakespeare in "A Midsummer Night's Dream." Titania herself appears in the transparent robe of silver gauze.

The reading of the "Poems in Prose" has often produced in us these impressions; a phrase, a word – one only – bizarrely chosen and placed, evoke for us an unknown world of forgotten and yet friendly faces. They revive the memories of early life, and present a mysterious choir of vanished ideas, murmuring in undertones among the phantoms of things apart from the realities of life. Other phrases, of a morbid tenderness, seem like music whispering consolation for unavowed sorrows and irremediable despair.

But it is necessary to beware, for such things as these make us homesick, like the "Ranz des vaches" of the poor Swiss lansquenet in the German ballad, in garrison at Strasbourg, who swam across the Rhine, was retaken and shot "for having listened too much to the sound of the horn of the Alps."

THÉOPHILE GAUTIER.

February 20th, 1868.

Charles Baudelaire by Etienne Carjat, 1863

Charles Baudelaire by Edouard Manet

SELECTED POEMS
OF CHARLES BAUDELAIRE

DONE INTO ENGLISH VERSE
BY GUY THORNE

PARFUM EXOTIQUE

Quand, les deux yeux fermés, en un soir chaud d'automne,
Je respire l'odeur de ton sein chaleureux,
Je vois se dérouler des rivages heureux
Qu'éblouissent les feux d'un soleil monotone;

Une île paresseuse où la nature donne
Des arbres singuliers et des fruits savoureux;
Des hommes dont le corps est mince et vigoureux,
Et des femmes dont l'œil, par sa franchise, étonne.

Guidé par ton odeur vers de charmants climats,
Je vois un port rempli de voiles et de mâts
Encor tout fatigués par la vague marine,

Pendant que le parfum des verts tamariniers,
Qui circule dans l'air et m'enfle la narine.
Se mêle dans mon âme au chant des mariniers.

EXOTIC PERFUME

(Parfum exotique)

With eve and Autumn in mine eyes confest,
I breathe an incense from thy heart of fire,
And happy hill-sides tired men desire
Unfold their glory in the weary West.

O lazy Isle! where each exotic tree
Is hung with delicate fruits, and slender boys
Mingle with maidens in a dance of joys
That knows not shame, where all are young and free.

Yes I thy most fragrant breasts have led me home
To this thronged harbour; and at last I know
Why searching sailors venture on the foam…

 – 'Tis that they may to Tamarisk Island go.
For there old slumberous sea-chants fill the air
Laden with spices, and the world is fair.

LE VIN DE L'ASSASSIN

Ma femme est morte, je suis libre!
Je puis donc boire tout mon soûl.
Lorsque je rentrais sans un sou,
Ses cris me déchiraient la fibre.

Autant qu'un roi je suis heureux;
L'air est pur, le ciel admirable…
 – Nous avions un été semblable
Lorsque je devins amoureux!

 – L'horrible soif qui me déchire
Aurait besoin pour s'assouvir
D'autant de vin qu'en peut tenir
Son tombeau; – ce n'est pas peu dire

Je l'ai jetée au fond d'un puits,
Et j'ai même poussé sur elle
Tous les pavés de la margelle.
 – Je l'oublierai si je le puis!

Au nom des serments de tendresse,
Dont rien ne peut nous délier,
Et pour nous réconcilier
Comme au beau temps de notre ivresse,

J'implorai d'elle un rendez-vous,
Le soir, sur une route obscure,
Elle y vint! folle créature!
 – Nous sommes tous plus ou moins fous!

Elle était encore jolie,
Quoique bien fatiguée! et moi,

Je l'aimai trop; – voilà pourquoi
Je lui dis: sors de cette vie!

Nul ne peut me comprendre. Un seul
Parmi ces ivrognes stupides
Songea-t-il dans ses nuits morbides
A faire du vin un linceul?

Cette crapule invulnérable
Comme les machines de fer,
Jamais, ni l'été ni l'hiver,
N'a connu l'amour véritable,

Avec ses noirs enchantements,
Son cortège infernal d'alarmes,
Ses fioles de poison, ses larmes,
Ses bruits de chaîne et d'ossements!

– Me voilà libre et solitaire!
Je serai ce soir ivre-mort;
Alors, sans peur et sans remord,
Je me coucherai sur la terre,

Et je dormirai comme un chien.
Le chariot aux lourdes roues
Chargé de pierres et de boues,
Le wagon enrayé peut bien

Ecraser ma tête coupable,
Ou me couper par le milieu,
Je m'en moque comme de Dieu,
Du Diable ou de la Sainte Table!

THE MURDERER'S WINE

(*Le vin de l'assassin*)

My wife is stiffened into wax.
    – Now I can drink my fill.
Her yellings tore my heart like hooks,
    They were so keen and shrill.'
'Tis a King's freedom that I know
    Since that loud voice is still.

The day is tender blue and gold,
    The sky is clear above …
Just such a summer as we had
    When first I fell in love.
… I'm a King now! Such royal thoughts
    Within me stir and move!

I killed her; but I could not slake
    My burning lava-wave
Of hideous thirst – far worse than that
    Of some long-tortured slave –
If I had wine enough to fill
    Her solitary, deep grave.

In slime and dark her body lies;
    It echoed as it fell.
(I will remember this no more.)
    Her tomb no man can tell.
I cast great blocks of stone on her,
    The curb-stones of the well.

We swore a thousand oaths of love;
    Absolved we cannot be

Nor ever reconciled, as when
    We both lived happily;
… 'Twas evening on a darkling road
    When the mad thing met me.

We all are mad, this I well think.
    … The madness of my wife
Was to come, tired and beautiful,
    To a madman with a knife!
I loved her far too much, 'twas why
    I hurried her from life.

I am alone among my friends,
    And of our sodden crowd
No single drunkard understands
    I sit apart and vowed.
They do not weave all night, and throw
    Wine-shuttles through a shroud!

True love has black enchantments; chains
    That rattle, and damp fears;
Wan phials of poison, dead men's bones,
    And horrible salt tears.
Of this the iron-bound drunkard knows
    Nothing, nor nothing hears.

I am alone. My wife is dead,
    And dead-drunk will I be
This self-same night, a clod on earth
    With naught to trouble me.
A dog I'll be, in a long dog-sleep,
    Oblivious and free!

The chariot with heavy wheels
    Comes rumbling through the night.

Crushed stones and mud are on its wheels,
    It is a thing of might!
The wain of retribution moves
    Slowly, as is most right.

It comes, to crack my guilty head
    Or crush my belly through,
I care not who the driver is;
    God and the devil too
 – Sitting side by side – can do no more
    Than that they needs must do!

LA MUSIQUE

La musique souvent me prend comme une mer!
   Vers ma pâle étoile,
Sous un plafond de brume ou dans un vaste éther,
   Je mets à la voile;

La poitrine en avant et les poumons gonflés
   Comme de la toile,
J'escalade le dos des flots amoncelés
   Que la nuit me voile;

Je sens vibrer en moi toutes les passions
   D'un vaisseau qui souffre;
Le bon vent, la tempête et ses convulsions

   Sur l'immense gouffre
Me bercent. – D'autres fois, calme plat, grand mimoir
   De mon désespoir!

MUSIC

(La Musique)

Music can lead me far, and far
    O'er mystical sad seas,
Where burns my pale, high-hanging star
    Among the mysteries
        Of Pleiades.

My lungs are taut of sweet salt air;
    The pregnant sail-cloths climb
The long, gloom-gathering ocean stair.
    I don the chord-shot cloak of Time
        While the waves chime!

Fierce winds and sombre tempests come
    And bludgeon heavily
All our vibrating timbers … drum
    Most passionately. O Sea!
        Liberate me!

So shall thy mighty void express
    Both depths and surface. There
Opens thy magic mirror; men confess
    To Thee their sick despair
        … No otherwhere.

LE JEU

Dans des fauteuils fanés des courtisanes vieilles,
Pâles, le sourcil peint, l'œil câlin et fatal,
Minaudant, et faisant de leurs maigres oreilles
Tomber un cliquetis de pierre et de métal;

Autour des verts tapis des visages sans lèvre,
Des lèvres sans couleur, des mâchoires sans dent,
Et des doigts convulsés d'une infernale fièvre,
Fouillant la poche vide ou le sein palpitant;

Sous de sales plafonds un rang de pâles lustres
Et d'énormes quinquets projetant leurs lueurs
Sur des fronts ténébreux de poètes illustres
Qui viennent gaspiller leurs sanglantes sueurs:

– Voilà le noir tableau qu'en un rêve nocturne
Je vis se dérouler sous mon œil clairvoyant,
Moi-même, dans un coin de l'antre taciturne,
Je me vis accoudé, froid, muet, enviant,

Enviant de ces gens la passion tenace,
De ces vieilles putains la funèbre gaîté,
Et tous gaillardement trafiquant à ma face,
L'un de son vieil honneur, l'autre de sa beauté!

Et mon cœur s'effraya d'envier maint pauvre homme
Courant avec ferveur à l'abîme béant,
Et qui, soûl de son sang, préférerait en somme
La douleur à la mort et l'enfer au néant!

THE GAME

(*Le jeu*)

In faded chairs old courtesans
  With painted eyebrows leer.
The stones and metal rattle in
  Each dry and withering ear,
As lackadaisical they loll,
  And preen themselves, and peer.

Their mumbling gums and lipless masks
  – Or lead-white lips – are prest
Around the table of green cloth;
  And withered hands, possest
Of Hell's own fever, vainly search
  In empty purse or breast.

Beneath the low, stained ceiling hang
  Enormous lamps, which shine
On the sad foreheads of great poets
  Glutted with things divine,
Who throng this ante-room of hell
  To find the anodyne.

I see these things as in a dream,
  With the clairvoyant eye,
And in a cottier of the den
  A crouching man descry;
A silent, cold, and envying man
  Who watches. It is I!

I envy those old harlots' greed
  And gloomy gaiety;

The gripping passion of the game,
　　The fierce avidity
With which men stake their honour for
　　A ruined chastity.

I dare not envy many a man:
　　Who runs his life-race well;
Whose brave, undaunted peasant blood
　　Death's menace cannot quell.
Abhorring *nothingness,* and strong
　　Upon the lip of Hell.

LE MAUVAIS MOINE

Les cloîtres anciens sur les grandes murailles
Étalaient en tableaux la sainte Vérité,
Dont l'effet, réchauffant les pieuses entrailles,
Tempérait la froideur de leur austérité.

En ces temps où du Christ florissaient les semailles
Plus d'un illustre moine, aujourd'hui peu cité,
Prenant pour atelier le champ des funérailles,
Glorifiait la Mort avec simplicité.

Mon âme est un tombeau que, mauvais cénobite,
Depuis l'éternité je parcours et j'habite;
Rien n'embellit les murs de ce cloître odieux.

O moine fainéant! quand saurai-je donc faire
Du spectacle vivant de ma triste misère
Le travail de mes mains et l'amour de mes yeux?

THE FALSE MONK

(*Le mauvais moine*)

Upon the tall old cloister walls there were
    Some painted frescoes showing Truth; so we,
Seeing them thus so holy and so fair,
    Might for a space forget austerity.

For when the Lord Christ's seeds were blossoming,
    Full many a simple, pious brother found
Death but a painted phantom with no sting,
    – And took for studio a burial-ground.

But my soul is a sepulchre, where I,
    A false Franciscan, dwell eternally,
And no walls glow with pictured mysteries.

When shall I rise from living death, to take
    My pain as rich material, and make
Work for my hands, with pleasure for mine eyes?

L'IDEAL

Ce ne seront jamais ces beautés de vignettes,
Produits avariés, nés d'un siècle vaurien,
Ces pieds à brodequins, ces doigts à castagnettes,
Qui sauront satisfaire un cœur comme le mien.

Je laisse, à Gavarni, poète des chloroses,
Soa troupeau gazouillant de beautés d'hôpital,
Car je ne puis trouver parmi ces pâles roses
Une fleur qui ressemble à mon rouge idéal.

Ce qu'il faut à ce cœur profond comme un abîme,
C'est vous, Lady Macbeth, âme puissante au crime,
Rêve d'Eschyle éclos au climat des autans;

Ou bien toi, grand Nuit, fille de Michel-Ange,
Qui tors paisiblement dans une pose étrange
Tes appas façonnés aux bouches des Titans!

AN IDEAL OF LOVE

(L'Idéal)

I hate those beauties in old prints,
    Those faded, simpering, slippered pets;
Vignetted in a room of chintz,
    And clacking silly castanets.

I leave Gavarni all his dolls,
    His sickly harems, pale and wan,
The beauties of the hospitals
    I do not wish to look upon.

Red roses are the roses real!
    Among the pale and virginal
Sad flowers, I find not my ideal
    … Vermilion or cardinal!

The panther-women hold my heart –
    Macbeth's dark wife, of men accurst,
… A dream of Æschylus thou art,
    'Tis such as thou shall quench my thirst!

… Or Michelangelo's daughter, Night,
    Who broods on her own beauty, she
For whose sweet mouth the Giants fight,
    Queen of my ideal love shall be!

L'AME DU VIN

Un soir, l'âme du vin chantait dans les bouteilles:
«Homme, vers toi je pousse, ô cher déshérité,
Sous ma prison de verre et mes cires vermeilles,
Un chant plein de lumière et de fraternité!

«Je sais combien il faut, sur la colline en flamme,
De peine, de sueur et de soleil cuisant
Pour engendrer ma vie et pour me donner l'âme;
Mais je ne serai point ingrat ni malfaisant,

«Car j'éprouve une joie immense quand je tombe
Dans le gosier d'un homme usé par ses travaux,
Et sa chaude poitrine est une douce tombe
Où je me plais bien mieux que dans mes froids caveaux.

«Entends-tu retentir les refrains des dimanches
Et l'espoir qui gazouille en mon sein palpitant?
Les coudes sur la table et retroussant tes manches,
Tu me glorifieras et tu seras content;

«J'allumerai les yeux de ta femme ravie;
A ton fils je rendrai sa force et ses couleurs
Et serai pour ce frêle athlète de la vie
L'huile qui raffermit les muscles des lutteurs.

«En toi je tomberai, végétale ambroisie,
Grain précieux jeté par l'éternel Semeur,
Pour que de notre amour naisse la poésie
Qui jaillira vers Dieu comme une rare fleur!»

THE SOUL OF WINE

(*L'Âme du vin*)

Vermilion the seals of my prison,
    Cold crystal its walls, and my voice
Singeth loud through the evening; a vision
    That bid'st thee rejoice!

Disinherited! outcast! – I call thee
    To pour, and my song in despite
Of the World shall enfold and enthrall thee
    Pulsating with light!

Long labours, fierce ardours, and blazing
    Of suns on far hill-sides, and strife
Of the toilers have gone to the raising
    Of me into life!

I forget not their pains, for I render
    Rewards; yea! in full-brimming bowl
To those who have helped to engender
    My passionate soul!

My joys are unnumbered, unending,
    When I rise from chill cellars to lave
The hot throat of Labour, ascending
    As one from the grave.

The Sabbath refrains that thou hearest,
    The whispering hope in my breast,
Shalt call thee, dishevelled and dearest!
    To ultimate rest.

The woman thy youthfulness captured,
    Who bore thee a son – this thy wife –
I will give back bright eyes, which enraptured
    Shall see thee as Life!
Thy son, a frail athlete, I dower
    With all my red strength, and the toil
Of his life shall be king-like in power,
    … Anointed with oil!

To thee I will bow me, thou fairest
    Gold grain from the Sower above.
Ambrosia I wedded, and rarest
    The fruits of our love.
High God round His feet shall discover
    The verses I made, in the hours
When I was thy slave and thy lover,
    Press upwards like flowers!

PRIÈRE

Gloire et louange à toi, Satan, dans les hauteurs
Du Ciel, où tu régnas, et dans les profondeurs
De l'Enfer, où, vaincu, tu rêves en silence!
Fais que mon âme un jour, sous l'Arbre de Science,
Près de toi se repose, à l'heure où sur ton front
Comme un Temple nouveau ses rameaux s'épandront!

THE INVOCATION

(Prière)

Glory to thee, Duke Satan. Reign
    O'er kings and lordly state.
Prince of the Powers of the Air
    And Hell; most desolate,
Dreaming Thy long, remorseful dreams
    And reveries of hate!

O let me lie near thee, and sleep
    Beneath the ancient Tree
Of Knowledge, which shall shadow thee
    Beelzebub, and me!
While Temples of strange sins upon
    Thy brows shall builded be.

LE CHAT

Viens, mon beau chat, sur mon cœur amoureux;
Retiens les griffes de ta patte,
Et laisse-moi plonger dans tes beaux yeux,
Mêlés de métal et d'agate.

Lorsque mes doigts caressent à loisir
Ta tête et ton dos élastique,
Et que ma main s'enivre du plaisir
De palper ton corps électrique,

Je vois ma femme en esprit. Son regard,
Comme le tien, aimable bête,
Profond et froid, coupe et fend comme un dard,

Et, des pieds jusques à la tête,
Un air subtil, un dangereux parfum
Nagent autour de son corps brun.

THE CAT

(Le Chat)

Most lovely, lie along my heart,
Within your paw your talons fold,
Let me find secrets in your eyes –
Your eyes of agate rimmed with gold!

For when my languid fingers move
Along your rippling back, and all
My senses tingle with delight
In softness so electrical,

My wife's face flashes in my mind;
Your cold, mysterious glances bring,
Sweet beast, strange memories of hers
That cut and flagellate and sting!

From head to foot a subtle air
Surrounds her body's dusky bloom,
And there attends her everywhere
A faint and dangerous perfume.

LE REVENANT

Comme les anges à l'œil fauve,
Je reviendrai dans ton alcôve
Et vers toi glisserai sans bruit
Avec les ombres de la nuit;

Et je te donnerai, ma brune,
Des baisers froids comme la lune
Et des caresses de serpent
Autour d'une fosse rampant.

Quand viendra le matin livide,
Tu trouveras ma place vide,
Où jusqu'au soir il fera froid.

Comme d'autres par la tendresse,
Sur ta vie et sur ta jeunesse,
Moi, je veux régner par l'effroi!

THE GHOST

(Le Revenant)

With some dark angel's flaming eyes
    That through the shadows burn,
Gliding towards thee, noiselessly,
    – 'Tis thus I shall return.

Such kisses thou shalt have of me
    As the pale moon-rays give,
And cold caresses of the snakes,
    That in the trenches live.

And when the livid morning comes,
    All empty by thy side,
And bitter cold, thou'lt find my place;
    Yea, until eventide.

Others young love to their embrace
    By tenderness constrain,
But over all thy youth and love
    I will by terror reign.

LES LITANIES DE SATAN

O toi, le plus savant et le plus beau des Anges,
Dieu trahi par le sort et privé de louanges,

O Satan, prends pitié de ma longue misère!

O Prince de l'exil, à qui l'on a fait tort,
Et qui, vaincu, toujours te redresses plus fort,

O Satan, prends pitié de ma longue misère!

Toi qui sais tout, grand roi des choses souterraines,
Guérisseur familier des angoisses humaines,

O Satan, prends pitié de ma longue misère!

Toi qui, même aux lépreux, aux parias maudits,
Enseignes par l'amour le goût du Paradis,

O Satan, prends pitié de ma longue misère!

O toi, qui de la Mort, ta vieille et forte amante,
Engendras l'Espérance, – une folle charmante!

O Satan, prends pitié de ma longue misère!

Toi qui fais au proscrit ce regard calme et haut
Qui damne tout un peuple autour d'un échafaud,

O Satan, prends pitié de ma longue misère!

Toi qui sais en quel coin des terres envieuses
Le Dieu jaloux cacha les pierres précieuses,

O Satan, prends pitié de ma longue misère!

Toi dont l'œil clair connaît les profonds arsenaux
Où dort enseveli le peuple des métaux,

O Satan, prends pitié de ma longue misère!

Toi dont la large main cache les précipices
Au somnambule errant au bord des édifices,

O Satan, prends pitié de ma longue misère!

Toi qui, magiquement, assouplis les vieux os
De l'ivrogne attardé foulé par les chevaux,

O Satan, prends pitié de ma longue misère!

Toi qui, pour consoler l'homme frêle qui souffre,
Nous appris à mêler le salpêtre et le soufre.

O Satan, prends pitié de ma longue misère!

Toi qui poses ta marque, ô complice subtil,
Sur le front du Crésus impitoyable et vil,

O Satan, prends pitié de ma longue misère!

Toi qui mets dans les yeux et dans le cœur des filles
Le culte de la plaie et l'amour des guenilles,

O Satan, prends pitié de ma longue misère!

Bâton des exilés, lampe des inventeurs,
Confesseur des pendus et des conspirateurs,

O Satan, prends pitié de ma longue misère!

Père adoptif de ceux qu'en sa noire colère
Du Paradis terrestre a chassés Dieu le Père,
O Satan, prends pitié de ma longue misère!

LES LITANIES DE SATAN

O Satan, most wise and beautiful of all the angels,
God, betrayed by destiny and bereft of praise,
Have pity on my long misery!

Prince of Exile, who hast been trodden down and vanquished,
But who ever risest up again more strong,
O Satan, have pity on my long misery!

Thou who knowest all; Emperor of the Kingdoms
    that are below the earth,
Healer of human afflictions,
Have pity on my long misery!

Thou who in love givest the taste of Paradise
To the Leper, the Outcast and those who are accursed,
O Satan, have pity on my long misery!

O thou who, of Death, thy strong old mistress,
Hast begotten the sweet madness of Hope,
Have pity on my long misery!

Thou who givest outlaws serenity, and the pride
Which damns a whole people thronging round the scaffold,
O Satan, have pity on my long misery!

Thou who knowest in what corners of the envious earth
The jealous God hath hidden the precious stones,
Have pity on my long misery!

Thou whose clear eye knoweth the deep arsenals
Wherein the buried metals are sleeping,
O Satan, have pity on my long misery!

Thou whose great hand hideth the precipice
And concealeth the abyss from those who walk in sleep,
Have pity on my long misery!

Thou who by enchantment makest supple the bones
    of the drunkard
When he falleth under the feet of the horses,
O Satan, have pity on my long misery!

Thou who didst teach weak men and those who suffer
To mix saltpetre and sulphur,
Have pity on my long misery!

Thou, O subtle of thought! who settest thy mask
Upon the brow of the merciless rich man,
O Satan, have pity on my long misery!

Thou who fillest the eyes and hearts of maidens
With longing for trifles and the love of forbidden things,
Have pity on my long misery!

Staff of those in exile, beacon of those who contrive
    strange matters,
Confessor of conspirators and those who are hanged,
O Satan, have pity on my long misery!

Sire by adoption of those whom God the Father
Has hunted in anger from terrestrial paradise,
Have pity on my long misery!

LE GUIGNON

Pour soulever un poids si lourd,
Sisyphe, il faudrait ton courage!
Bien qu'on ait du cœur à l'ouvrage,
L'Art est long et le temps est court.

Loin des sépultures célèbres,
Vers un cimetière isolé,
Mon cœur, comme un tambour voilé,
Va battant des marches funèbres.

Maint joyau dort enseveli
Dans les ténèbres et l'oubli,
Bien loin des pioches et des sondes;

Mainte fleur épanche à regret
Son parfum doux comme un secret
Dans les solitudes profondes.

ILL-STARRED!

(Le Guignon)

To raise this dreadful burden as I ought
It needs thy courage, Sisyphus, for I
Well know how long is Art, and Life how short.
  – My soul is willing, but the moments fly.

Towards some remote churchyard without a name
In forced funereal marches my steps come;
Far from the storied sepulchres of fame.
  – My heart is beating like a muffled drum.

Full many a flaming jewel shrouded deep
In shadow and oblivion, lies asleep,
Safe from the toiling mattocks of mankind.

Sad faery blossoms secret scents distil
In trackless solitudes; nor ever will
The lone anemone her lover find!

Note. – It seems fairly obvious – and perhaps this is a discovery – that Baudelaire must have read Gray's "Elegy." As we know, he was a first-class English scholar, and whether he plagiarised or unconsciously remembered the most perfect stanza that Gray ever wrote, one can hardly doubt that the gracious music of the French was borrowed from or influenced by the no less splendid rhythm of –

"Full many a gem of purest ray serene
The dark unfathomed caves of ocean bear:

Full many a flower is born to blush unseen,
And waste its sweetness on the desert air."

ÉPIGRAPHE POUR UN LIVRE CONDAMNÉ

Lecteur paisible et bucolique,
Sobre et naïf homme de bien,
Jette ce livre saturnien,
Orgiaque et mélancolique.

Si tu n'as fait ta rhétorique
Chez Satan, le rusé doyen,
Jette! tu n'y comprendrais rien,
Ou tu me croirais hystérique.

Mais si, sans se laisser charmer,
Ton œil sait plonger dans les gouffres,
Lis-moi, pour apprendre à m'aimer;

Ame curieuse qui souffres
Et vas cherchant ton paradis,
Plains-moi!... Sinon, je te maudis!

LINES WRITTEN ON THE FLY-LEAF OF AN EXECRATED BOOK

(*Épigraphe pour un livre condamné*)

Sober, simple, artless man,
      In these pages do not look,
Melancholy lurks within,
      Sad and saturnine the book.

Cast it from thee. If thou know'st
      Not of that dark learnèd band,
Whom wise Satan rules as Dean;
      Throw! Thou would'st not understand.

Yet, if unperturbed thou canst,
      Standing on the heights above,
Plunge thy vision in the abyss
      – Read in me and learn to love.

If thy soul hath suffered, friend,
      And for Paradise thou thirst,
Ponder my devil-ridden song
      And pity me ... or be accurst!

LA FIN DE LA JOURNÉE

Sous une lumière blafarde
Court, danse et se tord sans raison
La Vie, impudente et criarde.
Aussi, sitôt qu'à l'horizon

La nuit voluptueuse monte,
Apaisant tout, même la faim.
Effaçant tout, même la honte,
Le Poète se dit: «Enfin!

Mon esprit, comme mes vertèbres,
Invoque ardemment le repos;
Le cœur plein de songes funèbres,

Je vais me coucher sur le dos
Et me rouler dans vos rideaux,
O rafraîchissantes ténèbres!»

THE END OF THE DAY

(La Fin de la journée)

Beneath a wan and sickly light
Life, impudent and noisy, sways;
Most meaningless in all her ways.
She dances like a bedlamite,

Until the far horizon grows
Big with sweet night, at last! whose name
Appeases hunger, soothes the shame
And sorrow that the poet knows.

My very bones seem on the rack;
My spirit wails aloud; meseems
My heart is thronged with funeral dreams.

I will lie down and round me wrap
The cool, black curtains of the gloom
That night hath woven in her loom.

LITTLE POEMS IN PROSE

LE FOU ET LA VÉNUS

Quelle admirable journée! Le vaste parc se pâme sous l'oeil brûlant du soleil, comme la jeunesse sous la domination de l'Amour.

L'extase universelle des choses ne s'exprime par aucun bruit; les eaux elles-mêmes sont comme endormies. Bien différente des fêtes humaines, c'est ici une orgie silencieuse.

On dirait qu'une lumière toujours croissante fait de plus en plus étinceler les objets; que les fleurs excitées brûlent du désir de rivaliser avec l'azur du ciel par l'énergie de leurs couleurs, et que la chaleur, rendant visibles les parfums, les fait monter vers l'astre comme des fumées.

Cependant, dans cette jouissance universelle, j'ai aperçu un être affligé.

Aux pieds d'une colossale Vénus, un de ces fous artificiels, un de ces bouffons volontaires chargés de faire rire les rois quand le Remords ou l'Ennui les obsède, affublé d'un costume éclatant et ridicule, coiffé de cornes et de sonnettes, tout ramassé contre le piédestal, lève des yeux pleins de larmes vers l'immortelle Déesse.

Et ses yeux disent: " – Je suis le dernier et le plus solitaire des humains, privé d'amour et d'amitié, et bien inférieur en cela au plus imparfait des animaux. Cependant je suis fait, moi aussi, pour comprendre et sentir l'immortelle Beauté! Ah! Déesse! ayez pitié de ma tristesse et de mon délire!"

Mais l'implacable Vénus regarde au loin je ne sais quoi avec ses yeux de marbre.

VENUS AND THE FOOL

How glorious the day! The great park swoons beneath the Sun's burning eye, as youth beneath the Lordship of Love.

Earth's ecstasy is all around, the waters are drifting into sleep. Silence reigns in nature's revel, as sound does in human joy. The waning light casts a glamour over the world. The sun-kissed flowers plume the day with colour, and fling incense to the winds. They desire to rival the painted sky.

Yet, amidst the rout, I see one sore afflicted thing. A motley fool, a willing clown who brings laughter to the lips of kings when weariness and remorse oppress them; a fool in a gaudy dress, coiffed in cap and bells, huddles at the foot of a huge Venus. His eyes are full of tears, and raised to the goddess they seem to say:

"I am the last and most alone of mortals, inferior to the meanest animal, in that I am denied either love or friendship. Yet I, even I, am made for human sympathy and the adoration of immortal Beauty. O Goddess, have pity, have mercy on my sadness and despair."

But the implacable Venus stares through the world with her steady marble eyes.

LE DÉSIR DE PEINDRE

Malheureux peut-être l'homme, mais heureux l'artiste que le désir déchire!

Je brûle de peindre celle qui m'est apparue si rarement et qui a fui si vite, comme une belle chose regrettable derrière le voyageur emporté dans la nuit. Comme il y a longtemps déjà qu'elle a disparu!

Elle est belle, et plus belle; elle est surprenante. En elle le noir abonde: et tout ce qu'elle inspire est nocturne et profond. Ses yeux sont deux antres où scintille vaguement le mystère, et son regard illumine comme l'éclair: c'est une explosion dans les ténèbres.

Je la comparerais à un soleil noir, si l'on pouvait concevoir un astre noir versant la lumière et le bonheur. Mais elle fait plus volontiers penser à la lune, qui sans doute l'a marquée de sa redoutable influence; non pas la lune blanche des idylles, qui ressemble à une froide mariée, mais la lune sinistre et enivrante, suspendue au fond d'une nuit orageuse et bousculée par les nuées qui courent; non pas la lune paisible et discrète visitant le sommeil des hommes purs, mais la lune arrachée du ciel, vaincue et révoltée, que les Sorcières thessaliennes contraignent durement à danser sur l'herbe terrifiée!

Dans son petit front habitent la volonté tenace et l'amour de la proie. Cependant, au bas de ce visage inquiétant, où des narines mobiles aspirent l'inconnu et l'impossible, éclate, avec une grâce inexprimable, le rire d'une grande bouche, rouge et blanche, et délicieuse, qui fait rêver au miracle d'une superbe fleur éclose dans un terrain volcanique.

Il y a des femmes qui inspirent l'envie de les vaincre et de jouir d'elles; mais celle-ci donne le désir de mourir lentement sous son regard.

THE DESIRE TO PAINT

Unhappy is the man, but happy the artist, to whom this desire comes.

I long to paint one woman. She has come to me but seldom, swiftly passing from my sight, as some beautiful, unforgettable object the traveller leaves behind him in the night. It is long ago since I saw her.

She is lovely, far more than that; she is all-sufficing. She is a study in black: all that she inspires is nocturnal and profound. Her eyes are two deep pools wherein mystery vaguely coils and stirs; her glance is phosphorescent; it is like lightning on a summer night of black velvet.

She is comparable to a great black Sun, if one could imagine a dark star brimming over with happiness and light. She stirs within one dreams of the moon, Night's Queen who casts spells upon her – not the white moon, that cold bride of summer idylls, but the sinister, intoxicating moon which hangs in the leaden vault of storm, among the driven clouds; not the pale, peaceful moon who visits the sleep of the pure; but the fiery moon, torn from the conquered heavens, before whom dance the witches of Thessaly.

Upon the brow determination sits; she is ever seeking whom she may enthrall. Her delicately curved and quivering nostrils breathe incense from unknown lands; a haunting smile lingers on her subtle lips – lips softer than sleep-laden poppy petals, kissed by the suns of tropic lands.

There are women who inspire one with the desire to woo and win. She makes me long to fall asleep at her feet, beneath her slow and steady gaze.

CHACUN SA CHIMIÈRE

Sous un grand ciel gris, dans une grande plaine poudreuse, sans chemins, sans gazon, sans un chardon, sans une ortie, je rencontrai plusieurs hommes qui marchaient courbés.

Chacun d'eux portait sur son dos une énorme Chimère, aussi lourde qu'un sac de farine ou de charbon, ou le fourniment d'un fantassin romain.

Mais la monstrueuse bête n'était pas un poids inerte; au contraire, elle enveloppait et opprimait l'homme de ses muscles élastiques et puissants; elle s'agrafait avec ses deux vastes griffes à la poitrine de sa monture; et sa tête fabuleuse surmontait le front de l'homme, comme un de ces casques horribles par lesquels les anciens guerriers espéraient ajouter à la terreur de l'ennemi.

Je questionnai l'un de ces hommes, et je lui demandai où ils allaient ainsi. Il me répondit qu'il n'en savait rien, ni lui, ni les autres; mais qu'évidemment ils allaient quelque part, puisqu'ils étaient poussés par un invincible besoin de marcher.

Chose curieuse à noter: aucun de ces voyageur n'avait l'air irrité contre la bête féroce suspendue à son cou et collée à son dos; on eût dit qu'il la considérait comme faisant partie de lui-même. Tous ces visages fatigués et sérieux ne témoignaient d'aucun désespoir; sous la coupole spleenétique du ciel, les pieds plongés dans la poussière d'un sol aussi désolé que ce ciel, ils cheminaient avec la physionomie résignée de ceux qui sont condamnés à espérer toujours.

Et le cortège passa à côté de moi et s'enfonça dans l'atmosphère de l'horizon, à l'endroit où la surface arrondie de la planète se dérobe à la curiosité du regard humain.

Et pendant quelques instants je m'obstinai à vouloir comprendre ce mystère; mais bientôt l'irrésistible Indifférence s'abattit sur moi, et j'en fus plus lourdement accablé qu'ils ne l'étaient eux-mêmes par leurs écrasantes Chimères.

EACH MAN HIS OWN CHIMÆRA

Beneath a vault of livid sky, upon a far-flung and dusty plain where no grass grew, where not a nettle or a thistle dared raise its head, men passed me bowed down to the ground.

Each bore upon his back a great Chimæra, heavy as a sack of coal, or as the equipment of a foot-soldier of Rome.

But the monster was no dead weight. With her all-powerful and elastic muscles she encircled and oppressed her mount, clawing with two great talons at his breast. Her fabulous head reposed upon his brow, like a casque of ancient days whereby warriors struck fear to the hearts of their foes.

I questioned one of the wayfarers, asking why they walked thus. He replied that he knew nothing, neither he nor his companions, but that they moved towards an unknown land, urged on by irresistible impulse.

None of the wayfarers was discomforted by the foul thing which hung upon his neck. One said that it was part of himself.

Beneath the lowering dome of sky they journeyed on. They trod the dust-strewn earth – earth as desolate as the dusty sky. Their weary faces bore no witness to despair; they were condemned to hope for ever. So the pilgrimage passed and faded into the mist of the horizon, where the planet unveils itself to the human eye.

For some moments I tried to solve this mystery; but unconquerable Indifference fell upon me. And I was no more dejected by my burden than they by their crushing Chimæras.

ENIVREZ-VOUS

Il faut être toujours ivre. Tout est là: c'est l'unique question. Pour ne pas sentir l'horrible fardeau du Temps qui brise vos épaules et vous penche vers la terre, il faut vous enivrer sans trêve.

Mais de quoi? De vin, de poésie ou de vertu, à votre guise. Mais enivrez-vous.

Et si quelquefois, sur les marches d'un palais, sur l'herbe verte d'un fossé, dans la solitude morne de votre chambre, vous vous réveillez, l'ivresse déjà diminuée ou disparue, demandez au vent, à la vague, à l'étoile, à l'oiseau, à l'horloge, à tout ce qui fuit, à tout ce qui gémit, à tout ce qui roule, à tout ce qui chante, à tout ce qui parle, demandez quelle heure il est; et le vent, la vague, l'étoile, l'oiseau, l'horloge, vous répondront: "Il est l'heure de s'enivrer! Pour n'être pas les esclaves martyrisés du Temps, enivrez-vous; enivrez-vous sans cesse! De vin, de poésie ou de vertu, à votre guise."

INTOXICATION

To be drunken for ever: that is the only thing which matters! If you would escape Time's bruises and his heavy burdens which weigh you to the earth, you must be drunken.

But how? With the fruit of the wine, with poetry, with virtue, with what you will. But be drunken. And if, sometime, at the gates of a palace, on the green banks of a river, or in the shadowed loneliness of your own room, you should awake and find intoxication lessened or passed away, ask of the wind, of the wave, of the star, of the bird, of the timepiece; ask all that flies, all that sighs, all that revolves, all that sings, all that speaks – ask of these the hour. And the wind, the wave, the star, the bird, and the timepiece will answer you: "It is the hour to be drunken! Lest you be martyred slaves of Time, intoxicate yourselves, be drunken without cease! With wine, with poetry, with virtue, or with what you will."

LE GALANT TIREUR

Comme la voiture traversait le bois, il la fit arrêter dans le voisinage d'un tir, disant qu'il lui serait agréable de tirer quelques balles pour tuer le Temps. Tuer ce monstre-là, n'est-ce pas l'occupation la plus ordinaire et la plus légitime de chacun? – Et il offrit galamment la main à sa chère, délicieuse et exécrable femme, à cette mystérieuse femme à laquelle il doit tant de plaisirs, tant de douleurs, et peut-être aussi une grande partie de son génie.

Plusieurs balles frappèrent loin du but proposé; l'une d'elles s'enfonça même dans le plafond; et comme la charmante créature riait follement, se moquant de la maladresse de son époux, celui-ci se tourna brusquement vers elle, et lui dit: "Observez cette poupée, là-bas, à droite, qui porte le nez en l'air et qui a la mine si hautaine. Eh bien! cher ange, Je me figure que c'est vous." Et il ferma les yeux et il lâcha la détente. La poupée fut nettement décapitée.

Alors s'inclinant vers sa chère, sa délicieuse, son exécrable femme, son inévitable et impitoyable Muse, et lui baisant respectueusement la main, il ajouta: "Ah! mon cher ange, combien je vous remercie de mon adresse!"

As the carriage passed through the wood he told the driver to halt at a shooting-gallery, saying that he wished to have a few shots to kill time.

Is not the slaying of the monster Time the most usual and legitimate occupation of man?

So he graciously offered his hand to his dear, adorable, accursed wife; the mysterious woman who was his inspiration, to whom he owed many of his sorrows, many of his joys.

Several bullets went wide of the mark; one flew far away into the distance. His charming wife laughed deliriously, mocking at his clumsiness. Turning to her, he said brusquely:

"Look at that doll yonder, on your right, with its nose turned up and so supercilious an air. Think, sweet angel, I will picture to myself that it is you."

He closed his eyes, he pulled the trigger. The doll's head fell upon the ground.

Then, bending over his dear, adorable, accursed wife, his inevitable and merciless muse, he kissed her hand respectfully, and said: "Ah, sweet Angel, how I thank you for my skill!"

CORRESPONDENCE OF
CHARLES BAUDELAIRE

Baudelaire to Sainte-Beuve

19th March, 1856.

Here, my dear patron, is a kind of literature which will not, perhaps, inspire you with as much enthusiasm as it does me, but which will most surely interest you. It is necessary – that is to say that I desire, that Edgar Poe, who is not very great in America, should become a great man in France. Knowing how brave you are and what a lover of novelty, I have boldly promised your support to Michel Lévy.

Can you write me a line telling me if you will do something in the "Athenæum" or elsewhere? Because, in that case, I would write to M. Lalanne not to entrust this to any one else – your pen having a peculiar authority of which I am in need.

You will see at the end of the Notice (which contradicts all the current opinions in the United States) that I announce new studies. I shall speak of the opinions of this singular man later, in the matter of sciences, philosophy, and literature.

I deliver my always troubled soul into your hands.

Baudelaire to Sainte-Beuve

Wednesday, 26th March, 1856.

You well knew that this scrap of good news would enchant me. Lalanne had been warned by

Asselineau, and it would have been necessary for the book to have been given to another person if you had not been able to write the article. Lalanne has received a volume.

I can, with respect to the remainder of your letter, give you some details which will perhaps interest you.

There will be a second volume and a second preface. The first volume is written to draw the Public: "Juggling, hypotheses, false rumours," etc. "Ligeia" is the only important piece which is morally connected with the second volume.

The second volume is more markedly fantastic: "Hallucinations, mental maladies, pure grotesqueness, the supernatural," etc.

The second Preface will contain the analysis of the words that I shall not translate, and, above all, the statement of the scientific and literary opinions of the author. It is even necessary that I should write to M. de Humboldt on this subject to ask him his opinion on a little book which is dedicated to him; it is "Eureka."

The first preface, that you have seen and in which I have tried to comprise a lively protestation against Americanism, is almost complete from the biographical point of view. We shall pretend to wish to consider Poe only as a juggler, but I shall come back at the finish to the supernatural character of his poetry and his stories. He is only American in so far as he is a juggler. Beyond that, the thought is almost anti-American. Besides, he has made fun of his compatriots as much as he could.

Now, the piece to which you allude makes part of the second volume. It is a dialogue between two souls, after the destruction of the earth. There are three dialogues of this kind that I shall be happy to lend you at the end of the month, before delivering my second volume to the printer.

Now, I thank you with all my heart; but you are so kind that you run risks with me. After the Poe will come two volumes of mine, one of critical articles and the other of poems. Thus, I make my excuses to you beforehand; and, besides, I fear that when I shall no longer speak with the voice of a great poet, I shall be for you a brawling and disagreeable being.

Yours ever.

At the end of the second volume of Poe I shall put some

specimens of poetry.

I am persuaded that a man so careful as yourself would not wish me to ask him to take note of the orthography of the name [Edgar Poe]. No "d," no diæresis, no accent.

Baudelaire to Sainte-Beuve

9th March, 1857.

My dear friend, you are too indulgent to have taken exception to the impertinent point of interrogation that I have put after the word "souvenir" on the copy of the "Nouvelles histoires extra-ordinaires," that I laid aside for you yesterday at the "Moniteur." If you can be pleased, I shall think it very natural: you have spoilt me. If you cannot, I shall still find it very natural.

This second volume is of a higher and more poetic nature than two-thirds of the first. The third volume (in process of publication in the "Moniteur") will be preceded by a third notice.

The tale of the end of the world is called "Conversation of Eiros with Charmion."

A new pull has just been made of the first volume, in which the principal faults are corrected. Michel knows that he must keep a copy for you. If I have not the time to bring it to you, I shall have it sent to you.

Your affectionate.

Baudelaire to Sainte-Beuve

Wednesday, 18th August, 1857.

Ah! dear friend, I have something very serious, something very awkward to ask you. I wished to write to you, and then I would rather tell you. For a fortnight my ideas on this subject have been changing; but my lawyer (Chaix d'Est-Ange fils) insists that I talk to you about it, and I should be very happy if you could grant me a little conversation of three minutes to-day wherever you like, at your house or elsewhere. I did not wish to call on you unexpectedly. It always seems to me, when I take my way towards the rue Montparnasse, that I am going to visit that wonderful wise man, seated in a golden tulip, whose voice speaks to intruders with the resounding echo of a trumpet.

This morning I am awaiting some copies of my brochure; I will send you one at the same time.

Your very affectionate.

Baudelaire to Sainte-Beuve

Tuesday, 18th May, 1858.

I think that I drop in upon you as inconveniently as possible, do I not? You are engaged to-day; but, by coming to see you after four o'clock I shall perhaps be able to find you. In any case, whether I deceive myself or not, if you are busy this evening with your affairs, put me to the door like a true friend.

Yours always.

14*th June*, 1858.

DEAR FRIEND,

I have just read your work on "Fanny." Is there any need for me to tell you how charming it is and how surprising it is to see a mind at once so full of health, of herculean health, and at the same time most delicate, most subtle, most femininely fine! (On the subject of feminine fineness I wanted to obey you and to read the work of the stoic. In spite of the respect I ought to have for your authority, I decidedly do not wish that gallantry, chivalry, mysticism, heroism, in fact exuberance and excess, which are what is most charming even in honesty, should be suppressed.)

With you, it is necessary to be cynical; for you are too shrewd for deceit not to be dangerous. Ah well, this article has inspired me with terrible jealousy. So much has been said about Loëve-Weimars and of the service he has rendered to French literature! Shall I not find a champion who will say as much of me?

By some cajolery, most powerful friend, shall I obtain this from you? However, what I ask of you is not an injustice. Did you not offer it to me at first? Are not the "Adventures of Pym" an excellent pretext for a general sketch? You, who love to amuse yourself in all depths, will you not make an excursion into the depths of Edgar Poe? You guess that the request for this service is connected in my mind with the visit I must pay to M. Pelletier. When one has a little money and goes to dine with a former mistress one forgets everything. But there are days when the curses of all the fools mount to one's brain, and then one implores one's old friend, Sainte-Beuve.

Now, truly, of late I have been literally dragged in the mud, and (pity me, it is the first time that I have lacked dignity), I have had the weakness to reply.

I know how busy you are and how full of application for all your lessons, for all your work and duties, etc. But if, sometimes, a little strain were not put on friendliness, on kindness, where would the hero of friendliness be? And if one did not say too much good about brave men, how would they be consoled for the curses of those who only wish to say too much evil?

Finally, I will say to you, as usual, that all that you wish will be good.

Yours ever.

I like you more than I like your books.

Baudelaire to Sainte-Beuve

14th August, 1858.

Is it permitted to come and warm and fortify oneself a little by contact with you? You know what I think of men who are depressants and men who have a tonic influence. If, then, I unsettle you, you must blame your qualification, still more my weakness. I have need of you as of a douche.

Baudelaire to Sainte-Beuve

21st February, 1859.

My dear friend, I do not know if you take in the "Revue française." But, for fear that you should read it, I protest against a certain line (on the subject of "The Flowers of Evil"), page 171, in which the author – who, however, is very intelligent – is guilty of some injustice towards you.

Once, in a newspaper, I have been accused of ingratitude towards two chiefs of ancient romanticism *to whom I owe all*; it spoke, besides, with a judicial air, of this infamous trash.

This time, in reading this unfortunate line, I said to myself: "Mon Dieu! Sainte-Beuve, who knows my fidelity, but who knows that I am connected with the author, will perhaps believe that I have been capable of prompting this passage." It is exactly the contrary; I have quarrelled with Babou many a time in order to persuade him that you would always do everything you ought and could do.

A short time ago I was talking to Malassis of this great friendship, which does me honour and to which I owe so much good advice. The monster left me no peace until I gave him the long letter that you sent me at the time of my lawsuit, and which will serve, perhaps, as a plan for the making of a Preface. New "Flowers" are done, and passably out of the ordinary. Here, in repose, fluency has come back to me. There is one of them ("Danse macabre") which ought to have appeared on the 15th, in the "Revue contemporaine...."

I have not forgotten your Coleridge, but I have been a month without receiving any books, and to run through the 2,400 pages of Poe is some small labour.

Sincerely yours, and write to me *if you have time*.

Honfleur, Calvados (this address is sufficient).

What has become of the old rascal? (d'Aurevilly).

Baudelaire to Sainte-Beuve

28th February, 1859.

My dear friend, I learn that you have asked Malassis to communicate to you what you wrote to me on the subject of the "Flowers." Malassis is a little astounded; furthermore, he is ill. There were two letters; one, a friendly, complimentary letter; the other, a scheme of the address that you gave to me on the eve of my lawsuit. As, one day, I was classifying papers with Malassis, he begged me to give him that, and when I told him I intended to make use of it (not by copying but by paraphrasing and developing it) he said to me: "All the more reason. You will always find it again at my house. If your printer had it, it could not get lost."

I even think I remember having said to Malassis: "If I had pleaded my cause myself and if I had known how to develop this thesis, that a lawyer could not understand, I should doubtless have been acquitted."

I understand absolutely nothing of this nonsense in the "Revue française." The manager, however, seems to be a very well-bred young man. Every one knows that you have rendered many services to men younger than yourself. How has M. M – – printed this without making representations to Babou and without finding out what prejudice he had towards me?

Malassis, on whom I had not counted at all, has also seen the passage, and his letter is still more severe than yours.

I am going to Paris on the 4th or 5th. It would be very kind of you to write a word to Mme. Duval, 22, rue Beautreillis, to let me know if and when you wish to see me. I shall stay at her house.

Yours sincerely.

Baudelaire to Sainte-Beuve

3rd or 4th March, 1859.

A thousand thanks for your excellent letter. It has reassured me, but I think you are too sensitive. If ever I attain as good a position as yours, I shall be a man of stone. I have just read a very funny article of the "rascal" on Chateaubriand and M. de Marcellus, his critic. He has not missed the over easy witticism: "Tu Marcellus eris!"

In replying to Babou (what was important to me was to assure myself that you did not believe me capable of a meanness) I think that you attribute too much importance to him. He gives me the impression of being one of those people who believe that the pen is made to play tricks with. Boys' tricks, school hoaxes.

Yours sincerely.

Baudelaire to Sainte-Beuve

1860.

DEAR FRIEND,

I am writing to you beforehand, for precaution, because I have so strong a presentiment that I shall not have the pleasure of finding you.

I wrote recently to M. Dalloz a letter couched as nearly as possible like the following:

"Render account of the 'Paradis artificiels'! I know Messrs. So-and-so, So-and-so, etc., on the 'Moniteur.'"

Reply of Dalloz:

"The book is worthy of Sainte-Beuve. (It is not I speaking.)

Pay a visit to M. Sainte-Beuve about it."

I should not have dared to think so. Numerous reasons, of which I guess part, perhaps estrange you from it, and perhaps also the book does not please you.

However, I have more than ever need of being upheld, and I ought to have given you an account of my perplexity.

All that has been said about this essay has not any common sense, absolutely none.

P.S. – A few days ago, but then for the pure need of seeing you, as Antæus had need of the Earth, I went to the rue Montparnasse. On the way I passed a gingerbread shop, and the fixed idea took hold of me that you must like gingerbread. Note that nothing is better in wine at dessert; and I felt that I was going to drop in on you at dinner-time.

I sincerely hope that you will not have taken the piece of gingerbread, encrusted with angelica, for an idle joke, and that you will have eaten it in all simplicity.

If you share my taste, I recommend you, when you can get it, English gingerbread, very thick, very black, so close that it has neither holes nor pores, full of ginger and aniseed. It is cut in slices as thin as roast beef, and can be spread with butter or preserve. Yours always. Love me well.... I am passing through a great crisis.

Baudelaire to Sainte-Beuve

End of January, 1862.

Still another service that I owe you! When will this end? And how shall I thank you?

The article had escaped me. That explains to you the delay

before beginning to write to you.

A few words, my dear friend, to paint for you the peculiar kind of pleasure that you have obtained for me. Many years ago I was very much wounded (but I said nothing) to hear myself spoken of as a churl, an impossible and crabbed man. Once, in a wicked journal, I read some lines about my repulsive ugliness, well designed to alienate all sympathy (it was hard for a man who has loved the perfume of woman so well). One day a woman said to me: "It is curious, you are very presentable; I thought that you were always drunk and that you smelt evilly." She spoke according to the tale.

Now, my friend, you have put all that right, and I am very grateful to you for it – I, who have always said that it was not sufficient to be wise, but that above all it was necessary to be agreeable.

As for what you call my Kamtschatka, if I often received encouragements as vigorous as that, I believe that I should have the strength to make an immense Siberia of it, but a warm and populous one. When I see your activity, your vitality, I am quite ashamed; happily, I have sudden leaps and crises in my character which replace, though very inadequately, the action of sustained willingness.

Must I, the incorrigible lover of the "Rayons jaunes" and of "Volupté," of Sainte-Beuve the poet and novelist, now compliment the journalist? How do you arrive at this certainty of pen which allows you to say everything and makes a game of every difficulty for you? This article is not a pamphlet, for it is a righteousness. One thing struck me, and that is that I found again there all your eloquence in conversation, with its good sense and its petulances.

Really, I should have liked to collaborate in it a little – forgive this pride – I should have been able to give you two or three enormities that you have omitted through ignorance. I will tell you all this in a good gossip.

Ah, and your Utopia! the great way of driving the "vague, so dear to great nobles," from elections! Your Utopia has given me a new pride. I, also, have done it, Utopia, reform; – is it an old revolutionary movement that drove me, also, long ago, to make schemes for a constitution? There is this great difference, that yours is quite viable and that perhaps the day is not far off when it will be adopted.

Poulet-Malassis is burning to make a pamphlet of your admirable article....

I ask you to promise to find some minutes to reply to the following:

Great trouble, the necessity of working, physical ills, have interfered with my proceedings.

At last I have fifteen examples of my principal books. My very restricted distribution list is made.

I think it is good policy to put up for the Lacordaire chair. There are no literary men there. It was first of all my own design, and, if I had not done so, it was not to disobey you and not to appear too eccentric. If you think my idea good, I will write a letter to M. Villemain before next Wednesday, in which I will briefly say that it seems to me that the choice of a candidate must not only be directed by the desire of success, but must also be a sympathetic homage to the memory of the deceased. Besides, Lacordaire is a romantic priest, and I love him. Perhaps I shall slur over the word "romantic" in the letter, but not without consulting you.

It is imperative that this terrible rhetorician, this so grave and unkindly man, should read my letter; this man who preaches while he talks, with the expression and the solemnity (but not with the good faith) of Mlle. Lenormand. I have seen this lady in the robe of a professor, set in her chair, like a Quasimodo, and she had over M. Villemain the advantage of a very sympathetic voice.

If, by chance, M. Villemain is dear to you, I at once take back all that I have just said; and, for love of you, I shall do my best to find him lovable.

However, I cannot help thinking that, as a papist, I am worth more than him ... even though I am a very-much-suspected Catholic.

I want, in spite of my tonsure and my white hairs, to speak to you as a little boy. My mother, who is very much bored, is continually asking me for novelties. I have sent her your article. I know what maternal pleasure she will draw from it. Thank you for me and for her.

Your very devoted.

Baudelaire to Sainte-Beuve

Monday evening, 3rd *February*, 1862.

My dear friend, I am trying hard to guess those hours which are your leisure hours, and I cannot succeed. I have not written a word, in accordance with your advice; but I am patiently continuing my visits, in order to let it be well understood that I want, with regard to the election in replacement of Father Lacordaire, to gather some votes from *men of letters*. I think that Jules Sandeau will speak to you about me; he has said to me very graciously: "You catch me too late, but I will go and find out if there is anything to be done for you."

Twice I have seen Alfred de Vigny, who has kept me three hours each time. He is an admirable and delightful man, but not fitted for action, and even dissuading from action. However, he has shown me the warmest sympathy.

You do not know that the month of January has been a month of fretfulness and neuralgia for me.... I say this in order to explain the interruption in my proceedings.

I have seen Lamartine, Patin, Viennet, Legouvé, de Vigny, Villemain (horror!), Sandeau. Really, I do not remember any others. I have not been able to find either Ponsard, or M. Saint-Marc Girardin, or de Sacy.

At last I have sent a few copies of some books to *ten* of those whose works I know. This week I shall see some of these gentlemen.

I have written an analysis, such as it is, of your excellent article (without signing it; but my conduct is infamous, is it not?) in the "Revue anecdotique" As for the article itself, I have sent it to M. de Vigny, who did not know it, and who showed me that he wished to read it.

As for the talkers of politics, among whom I shall not be able to find any pleasure, I shall go the round of them in a carriage. They shall have only my card and not my face.

This evening I have read your "Pontmartin." Pardon me for saying to you, "What lost talent!" In your prodigality there is at times something which scandalises me. It seems to me that I, after having said, "The most noble causes are sometimes upheld by bumpkins," I should have considered my work finished. But you have particular talents for suggestion and divination. Even towards the most culpable beasts you are delightfully polished. This Monsieur Pontmartin is a great hater of literature....

I have sent you a little parcel of sonnets. I will next send you several packets of reveries in prose, without counting a huge work on the "Painters of Morals" (crayon, water-colour, printing, engraving).

I do not ask you if you are well. That is sufficiently apparent.

I embrace you and shake you by the hands. – I leave your house.

Baudelaire to Sainte-Beuve

15*th March*, 1865.

Dear friend, I take advantage of the "Histoires grotesques et sérieuses" to remind myself of you. Sometimes, in the mornings, I talk about you with M. Muller, of Liège, by whose side I take luncheon, – and in the evening, after dinner, I am re-reading "Joseph Delorme" with Malassis. Decidedly, you are right; "Joseph Delorme" is the old woman's "Flowers of Evil." The comparison is glorious for me. Have the goodness not to find it offensive to yourself.

And the Preface of the "Vie de César?" Is it predestinarian enough?

Yours always.

BRUXELLES, RUE DE LA MONTAGNE, 28.

Baudelaire to Sainte-Beuve

Thursday, 30*th March*, 1865.

My dear friend, I thank you for your excellent letter; can you write any which are not excellent? When you call me "My dear son," you touch me and make me laugh at the same time. In spite of my many white hairs, which make me look (to the stranger) like an academician, I have great need of some one who loves me enough to call me his "son"; but I cannot help thinking of that burgrave of 120 years of age who, speaking to a burgrave of eighty, said to him: "Young man, be silent!" (In parentheses – and let this be between us – if I wrote a tragedy I should be afraid of letting fly some shafts of this energy and of hitting another target than that at which I had aimed.)

Only, I observe that in your letter there is no allusion to the copy of "Histoires grotesques et sérieuses" that I asked Michel Lévy to send you. I swear to you, besides, that I have no intention whatever of getting the least advertisement for this book out of you. My only aim was, knowing as you well know how to distribute your time, to provide you with an occasion for enjoying once more an amazing subtlety of logic and sensations. There are people who will find that the fifth volume is inferior to the preceding ones; but that is of no consequence to me.

We are not as bored as you think, Malassis and I. We have learnt to go without everything, in a country where there is nothing, and we have understood that certain pleasures (those of conversation, for example) grow in proportion as certain needs diminish.

On the subject of Malassis, I will tell you that I marvel at his courage, at his activity, and his incorrigible gaiety. He has arrived at a very surprising erudition in point of books and prints. Everything amuses him and everything teaches him. One of our chief amusements is when he pretends to play the atheist and when I try to play the Jesuit. You know that I can become religious by contradiction (above all here) so that, to make me impious, it would be sufficient to put me in contact with a slovenly curé (slovenly of body and soul). As for the publication of some humorous books which it has pleased him to amend with the same piety that he would have put at the service of Bossuet or Loyola, even I have drawn from them a little, little unexpected gain: *it is a clearer understanding of the French Revolution.* When people amuse themselves in a certain way, it is a good diagnosis of revolution.

Alexander Dumas has just left us. This fine man has come to show himself with his ordinary candour. In flocking round him to get a shake of the hand, the Belgians made fun of him.... That is unworthy. A man can be worthy of respect for his vitality. Vitality of the negro, it is true. But I think that many others, besides myself, lovers of the serious, have been carried away by "La Dame de Montsoreau" and by "Balsamo."

As I am very impatient to return to France, I have written to J. L. to commission him with my small affairs. I would like to collect, in three or four volumes, the best of my articles on the "Stimulants," the "Painters," and the "Poets," adding thereto a series of "Observations on Belgium." If, in one of your rare strolls, you go along the boulevard de Gand, stir up his good feeling a little and exaggerate what you think of me.

I must own that three important fragments are lacking, one on Didactic Painting (Cornélius, Kaulbach, Chenavard, Alfred Réthel), another, "Biography of the Flowers of Evil," and then a last: "Chateaubriand and his Family." You know that my passion for this old dandy is incorrigible. To sum up, little work; ten days perhaps. I am rich in notes.

Pardon me if I intrude in a delicate question; my excuse is my desire to see you content (supposing that certain things would content you) and to see every one do you justice. I hear many people saying, "What! Sainte-Beuve is not yet a senator?" Many years ago I said to E. Delacroix, to whom I could speak my mind, that many young men preferred to see him remaining in the state of an outcast and rebel. (I alluded to his stubbornness in presenting himself at the Institute.) He replied: "My dear sir, if my right arm was struck by paralysis, my capacity as member of the Institute would give me the right of teaching, and if I always keep well the Institute can serve to pay my coffee and cigars. In two words, I think that, with regard to you, it resolves itself into a certain accusation of ingratitude against the government of Napoleon, in many other minds besides mine." You forgive me, do you not? for violating the limits of discretion; you know how much I love you; and then I chatter like some one who rarely has an opportunity for talking.

I have just read Émile Ollivier's long discourse. It is very extraordinary. He speaks, it seems, with the authority of a man who has a great secret in his pocket.

Have you read Janin's abominable article against melancholy and mocking poets? And Viennet, quoted amongst the *great poets* of France! And a fortnight after, an article in favour of Cicero! Do they take Cicero for an Orleanist or an academician? M. de Sacy says: "Cicero is our Cæsar, ours!" Oh no, he is not, is he?

Your very affectionate.

Without any transition, I will tell you that I have just found an admirable melancholy ode by Shelley, composed on the shores of the Gulf of Naples, and which ends with these words: "I know that I am one of those whom men do not love; but I am one of those whom they remember." Very good! this is poetry!

Baudelaire to Sainte-Beuve

Thursday 4th May, 1865.

MY DEAR SAINTE-BEUVE, – As I take up a pen to write you some words of congratulation on your nomination, I find a letter that I wrote you on March 31st which has not yet gone, probably because of stupidity on my part or on the part of the hotel people.

I have read it again. I find it boyish, childish. But I send it to you just the same. If it makes you laugh, I shall not say "So much the worse," but "So much the better." I am not at all afraid, knowing your indulgence, to strip myself before you.

To the passage which treats of J. L. I shall add that I have finished the fragments in question (except the book on Belgium, which I have not the courage to finish here) and that, obliged to go to Honfleur to seek all the other pieces composing the books announced to L..., I shall doubtless go on to Paris on the 15th, in order to torment him a little. If, by chance, you see him, you can tell him.

As for Malassis, his terrible affair happens on the 12th, He thinks he is sure to be condemned to five years. The serious thing is that this closes France to him for five years. That this momentarily cuts off supplies, I do not think so great an evil. He will be constrained to do other things. It is more to count on the universal mind than to brave compulsory public decency. As for me, who am not a prude, I have never possessed one of these silly books, even printed in beautiful characters and with beautiful illustrations.

Alas! the "Poems in Prose" to which you have again sent a recent encouragement, are much delayed. I am always giving myself difficult work. To make a hundred laborious trifles which demand unfailing good-humour (good-humour necessary even to treat of sad subjects), a strange stimulant which needs sights, crowds, music, even street-lamps, that is what I wanted to do! I am only at sixty and I can go no further. I need this famous "bath of the multitude" of which the error has justly shocked you.

M. has come here. I have read your article. I have admired your suppleness and your aptitude to enter into the soul of all the talents. But to this talent there is something lacking which I cannot define. M. has gone to Anvers, where there are magnificent things – above all, examples of this monstrous, Jesuitical style which pleases me so much, and which I hardly know except from the chapel of the college at Lyons, which is made with different coloured marbles. Anvers has a museum of a very special kind, full of unexpected things, even for those who can put the Flemish school in its true place. Finally, this town has the grand, solemn air of an old capital, accentuated by a great river. I believe that this fine fellow has seen nothing of all this. He has only seen a fat fry that he has gone from the other side of the Escaut to eat. He is, nevertheless, a charming man.

Decidedly, I congratulate you with all my heart. You are now the equal (officially) of many mediocre people. That matters little. You wished it, did you not? need, perhaps? You are content, then

I am happy.

Yours always.

11th July, 1865.

Very dear friend, I could not cross Paris without coming to shake you by the hand. Very soon, probably in a month.

I saw J. L... three days ago, when I was making for Honfleur. L. pretended that he was going to undertake some important business for me with MM. G.... If you could intervene in my favour with one or two authoritative words, you would make me happy. You do not wish my awkward compliments on the subject of the Senate, do you?

Your very devoted friend.

I start again for the infernal regions to-morrow evening. Till then, I am at the Hôtel du chemin de fer du Nord. Place de Nord.

BRUXELLES,

Tuesday, 2*nd January*, 1866.

MY GOOD FRIEND,

I have just seen that, for the first time in your life, you have delivered your physical person to the public. I allude to a portrait of you published by "L'Illustration." It really is very like you!

The familiar, mocking, and rather concentrated expression, and the little calotte itself is not hidden. Shall I tell you I am so bored that this simple image has done me good? The phrase has an impertinent air. It means simply that, in the loneliness in which some old Paris friends have left me (J. L. in particular), your image has been enough to divert me from my weariness. What would I not give to go, in five minutes, to the rue Mont-Parnasse, to talk with you for an hour on your articles on Proudhon; with you who know how to listen even to men younger than yourself!

Believe me, it is not that I find the reaction in his favour illegitimate. I have read him a good deal and known him a little. Pen in hand, he was a *bon bougre*; but he was not, and would never have been, even on paper, a dandy. For that I shall never pardon him. And it is that that I shall express, were I to excite the ill-humour of all the great beasts, right-thinking, of the "Universe."

Of your work I say nothing to you. More than ever you have the air of a confessor and *accoucheur* of souls. They said the same thing of Socrates, I think; but Messrs. Baillarger and Lélut have declared, *on their conscience*, that he was mad.

This is the commencement of a year that will doubtless be as boring, as stupid, as criminal as all the preceding ones. What good can I wish you? You are virtuous and lovable, and (extraordinary thing!) they are beginning to do you justice!…

I chatter far too much, like a nervous man who is tired. Do not reply to me if you have not five minutes of leisure.

Your very affectionate.

Baudelaire to Sainte-Beuve

15th January, 1866.

My dear friend, I do not know how to thank you enough for your good letters. It is really all the kinder of you because I know you are very busy. If I am sometimes long in replying it is on the score of health, which prevents me and even sends me to bed for many days. I shall follow your advice: I shall go to Paris and I shall see the G...s myself. Then, perhaps, I shall commit the indiscretion of asking you to give me a helping hand. But when? For six weeks I have been immersed in a chemist's shop. If it should be necessary to give up beer, I do not ask anything better. Tea and coffee, that is more serious; but will pass. Wine? the devil! it is cruel. But here is a still harder creature who says I must neither read nor study. What a strange medicine is that which prohibits the principal function! Another tells me for all consolation that I am hysterical. Do you admire, like me, the elastic usage of these fine words, well chosen to cloak our ignorance of everything?

I have tried to plunge again into the "Spleen de Paris" ["Poems in Prose"], for that was not finished. Finally, I hope to be able to show, one of these days, a new Joseph Delorme, grappling with his rhapsodic thought at each incident in his stroll and drawing from each object a disagreeable moral. But how difficult it is to make nonsense when one wishes to express it in a manner at the same time impressive and light!

Joseph Delorme has arrived there quite naturally. I have taken up the reading of your poems again *ab ovo*. I saw with pleasure that at each turn of the page I recognised verses which are old friends. It appears that, when I was a boy, I had not such very bad taste. (The same thing happened to me in December with Lucain. "Pharsale," always glittering, melancholy, lacerating, stoical, has consoled my neuralgia. And this pleasure has led me to think that in reality we change very little. That is to say, that there is something invariable in us.)

Since you own that it does not displease you to hear your works spoken of, I am much tempted to write you thirty pages of confidences on this subject; but I think I should do better to write them first in good French for myself, and then to send them to a paper, if there still exists a journal in which one can talk poetry.

However, here are some suggestions of the book which came to me by chance.

I have understood, much better than heretofore, the "Consolations" and the "Pensées d'août."

I have noted as more brilliant the following pieces: "Sonnet à Mad. G...," page 225.

Then you knew Mme. Grimblot, that tall and elegant Russian for whom the word "désinvolture" was made and who had the hoarse, or rather the deep and sympathetic voice of some Parisian comediennes? I have often had the pleasure of hearing Mme. de Mirbel lecture her and it was very comical. (After all, perhaps I am deceiving myself; perhaps it is another Mme. G.... These collections of poetry are not only of poetry and psychology, but are also annals.) "Tu te révoltes" ... "Dans ce cabriolet" ... "En revenant du Convoi" ... "La voilà."...

Page 235, I was a little shocked to see you desiring the approbation of MM. Thiers, Berryer, Thierry, Villemain. Do these gentlemen really feel the thunderclap or the enchantment of an object of art? And are you then very much afraid of not being appreciated to have accumulated so many justificatory documents? To admire you, do I need the permission of M. de Béranger?

Good Heavens! I nearly forgot the "Joueur d'orgue," page 242. I have grasped much better than formerly the object and the art of narratives such as "Doudun," "Marèze," "Ramon," "M. Jean," etc. The word "analytical energy" applies to you much more than to André Chénier.

There is still one piece that I find marvellous: it is the account of a watch-night, by the side of an unknown corpse, addressed to Victor Hugo at the time of the birth of one of his sons.

What I call the decoration (landscape or furniture) is always perfect.

In certain places of "Joseph Delorme" I find a little too much of lutes, lyres, harps, and Jehovahs. This is a blemish in the Parisian poems. Besides, you have come to destroy all that. Indeed, pardon me! I ramble on! I should never have dared to talk to you so long about it.

I have found the pieces that I know by heart again. (Why should one reread, with pleasure, in printed characters, that which memory could recite?)

"Dans l'île de Saint-Louis" (Consolations).

"Le Creux de la Vallée," p. 113. Here is much of Delorme!

And "Rose" (Charming), p. 127.

"Stances de Kirke White" p. 139.

"La Plaine" (beautiful October landscape), p. 138.

Heavens! I must stop. I seem to pay you compliments, and I have no right. It is impertinent.

Baudelaire to Flaubert

Tuesday, 25th August, 1857.

Dear friend, I wrote you a hasty little note before five o'clock solely to prove to you my repentance at not having replied to your affectionate sentiments. But if you knew in what an abyss of puerile occupations I have been plunged! And the article on "Madame Bovary" is again deferred for some days! What an interruption in life is a ridiculous adventure!

The comedy is played on Thursday; it has lasted a long time. Finally, three hundred francs fine, two hundred francs for the editors, suppression of numbers 20, 30, 39, 80, 81 and 87. I will write to you at length to-night.

Yours always, as you know.

Baudelaire to Flaubert

26*th June*, 1860.

MY DEAR FLAUBERT, I thank you very much for your excellent letter. I was struck by your observation, and, having fallen very severely in the memory of my dreams, I perceived that, all the time, I was beset by the impossibility of rendering an account of certain actions or sudden thoughts of man, without the hypothesis of the intervention of an evil force outside himself. Here is a great confession for which the whole confederated nineteenth century shall not make me blush. Mark well that I do not renounce the pleasure of changing my opinion or of contradicting myself.

One of these days, if you permit it, in going to Honfleur I shall stop at Rouen; but, as I presume that you are like me and that you hate surprises, I shall warn you some time beforehand.

You tell me that I work well. Is it a cruel mockery? Many people, not counting myself, think that I do not do anything very great.

To work: that is to work without ceasing; that is to have no more feeling, no more dreaming; and it is to be pure volition always in action. I shall perhaps attain to it.

Always your very devoted friend.

I have always dreamed of reading (in its entirety) the "Tentation" and another strange book of which you have published no fragment (Novembre). And how goes Carthage?

Baudelaire to Flaubert

End of January, 1862.

MY DEAR FLAUBERT, I have committed an act of desperation, a madness, that I am changing into an act of wisdom by my persistence. If I had time enough (it would take very long) I would amuse you greatly by recounting my academical visits to you.

I am told that you are closely connected with Sandeau (who said, some time ago, to a friend of mine: "Oh, does M. Baudelaire write prose?"). I should be very much obliged if you would write to him what you think of me. I shall go and see him and will explain the meaning of this candidature which has surprised some of these gentlemen so much.

For a very long time I have wished to send you a brochure on Wagner, beyond which I do not know what to send. But, what is very absurd for a candidate, I have not one of my books with me at home.

On Monday last, in the "Constitutionnel" Sainte-Beuve wrote a masterly article, a pamphlet, enough to make one die with laughing, on the subject of candidates.

Always yours devotedly.

Baudelaire to Flaubert
PARIS,

31st January, 1862.

MY DEAR FLAUBERT,
You are a true warrior. You deserve to be in the Sacred

Legions. You have the blind faith of friendship, which implies the true statesman (sic).

But, good recluse, you have not read Sainte-Beuve's famous article on the Academy and the candidateships. This has been the talk for a week, and of necessity it has re-echoed violently in the Academy.

Maxime du Camp told me that I was disgraced, but I am persisting in paying my visits, although certain academicians have declared (can it be really true?) that they would not even receive me at their houses. I have committed a rash action of which I do not repent. Even if I should not obtain a single vote, I shall not repent of it. An election takes place on February 6th, but it is from the last one (Lacordaire, February 20th) that I shall try to snatch two or three votes. I think of myself alone (at least if it comes to a reasonable candidateship) in front of the ridiculous little Prince du Broglie, son of the duke, living academician. These people will end by electing their concierges, and those concierges are Orleanists.

Doubtless, we shall see each other soon. I dream always of solitude, and if I go away before your return I will pay you a visit for some hours down there.

How is it that you have not guessed that Baudelaire would rather be Auguste Barbier, Théophile Gautier, Banville, Flaubert, Leconte de Lisle – that is to say, pure literature? That was understood immediately by a few friends, and has gained me some sympathy.

Thank you and yours always.

Have you noticed that to write with a steel pen is like walking on unsteady stones with sabots?

Baudelaire to Flaubert
PARIS,

3rd February, 1862.

MY DEAR FRIEND,

M. Sandeau was charming, his wife was charming, and I really believe that I was as charming as they were, since we all held a concert in your honour, so harmonious that it was like a veritable trio performed by consummate artists.

As for my affairs, Sandeau reproached me for taking him unawares. I ought to have seen him sooner. However, he will speak for me to some of his friends at the Academy, "And perhaps – perhaps," said he, "I shall be able to snatch some Protestant votes in the ballot for the Lacordaire chair." It is everything I desire.

Seriously, Mme. Sandeau's enthusiasm is great, and in her you have an advocate, a more than zealous panegyrist. That greatly excited my rivalry, and I succeeded in finding some reasons for eulogy that she had forgotten.

Here is Sandeau's letter. Here is a little paper which will perhaps interest you.

Yours always. Hope to see you soon.

SOME REMARKS ON BAUDELAIRE'S INFLUENCE UPON MODERN POETRY AND THOUGHT

In his essay called "Pen, Pencil, and Poison" Oscar Wilde remarks: "But had the man worn a costume and spoken a language different from our own, had he lived in Imperial Rome, or at the time of the Italian Renaissance, or in Spain in the seventeenth century, or in any land or in any century but this century and this land, we should be quite able to arrive at a perfectly unprejudiced estimate of his position and value"; and he also says: "Of course, he is far too close to our own time for us to be able to form any purely artistic judgment about him."

It was only a year after the death of Charles Baudelaire that Gautier wrote the magnificent life-study of the poet, the English translation of which forms part of this volume, and the monograph seems to give the lie direct to Wilde's assertion. There is nothing finer in French literature, more delicately critical, more vivid in its personal pictures, more perfect in its prose. It is the triumph of a luminous brain, full of rays and ideas "whence images buzz forth like golden bees."

Yet it is just because there is some truth in Wilde's plea, that there is still something to be said to-day of Baudelaire. The attempt to say it may seem presumptuous, and I am certain that no single word of Gautier could be altered or improved upon. Everything fitted the biographer for his task. He knew Charles Baudelaire intimately. He possessed an ear for rhythm unequalled in its kind; his fervent and romantic fancy rendered him peculiarly able to appreciate the most delicate of Baudelaire's thoughts and tones of his music. Finally – a fact which has hitherto escaped notice in this connection – the "Mademoiselle de Maupin" of Gautier published in 1835 created much the same scandal and alarm as Baudelaire's "Les Fleurs du Mal" did in 1857. Although Théophile Gautier himself escaped the fate of being publicly prosecuted for an offence against public morals, he knew what it was to suffer a literary martyrdom, and could feel for his younger friend when the author of "Une Charogne" was brought before the Court. Indeed, it was in the very year that "Les Fleurs du Mal" was issued that Flaubert was prosecuted on account of "Madame Bovary" and Gautier became in consequence the great novelist's staunch friend and champion.

Gautier, above all his contemporaries, was of precisely the temper of mind to appreciate Charles Baudelaire. Nothing was lacking in the man, his temperament or his opportunities, to produce a masterpiece which, ranking with the "Voltaire" of Lord Morley, or Walter Pater's "Leonardo da Vinci" is almost unknown by the general English reader.

Yet there is much to be said of Baudelaire that Gautier could not say. Gautier died in 1872. At that time Baudelaire's work was only known to a distinguished literary coterie. In England it had hardly been heard of. Swinburne, in 1866, when "Poems and Ballads" appeared, was almost certainly the only English man of letters who understood the French poet.

Recently a certain amount has been written about Baudelaire in England. Oscar Wilde constantly refers to his poems; there have been some review articles for the making of which the writers have drawn largely upon Gautier and Asselineau's "Charles Baudelaire; sa vie et son œuvre." Mr. F. P. Sturm (in 1905) made a fine study of the poet as an introduction to an English verse translation of "Les Fleurs du Mal," published in the "Canterbury Poets" series. It is because I believe I have something new to say that I have dared to include a short study with my translations of Gautier's jewelled prose and of Baudelaire's poems.

Only a very few years ago in England, it was thought, though quite wrongly thought, that the more eclectic literary artists of England and France would, and must always, remain the peculiar property of the leisured and cultured classes. It was not only because the books of such writers were difficult of access and costly in price. Men and women privileged to enjoy and appreciate the work of Baudelaire or Verlaine in France, Walter Pater or Oscar Wilde in England, honestly believed that the vast mass of readers were temperamentally and by training unable to understand these and other artists.

The fact of compulsory education created a proletariat able and willing to read. Astute exploiters of popular necessity arose and began to supply cheap "reading matter" with all the aplomb and success that would have attended their efforts if they had been directed towards any other newly risen want. This happened a generation ago. Millions still feed upon the literary hogwash provided for them, but from among those millions a new class has arisen that asks for better fare, and does not ask in vain.

To take a single instance. Ruskin's works, in the "Everyman" library, are supplied at a shilling a volume. The demand has been enormous.

Again, a paper like "T.P.'s Weekly," costing a penny and dealing with the best things of literature, has an enormous circulation and a personal influence over hardworking middle-class men and women with little leisure for self-culture, that it is impossible to overrate.

Moreover, the issue of Oscar Wilde's finest work at a trifling price has been attended with a success that has startled no one more greatly than the adventurous publishers themselves.

Now these things are signs of the times. If they show anything at all, they show that the work of writers which has been hitherto thought to be far above the head of the ordinary reader is really not so in the least. And because I am persuaded that opportunity alone has been wanting, I have ventured upon this book.

Gautier's immortal essay takes the first place. We have here a piece of criticism and explanation which, while never digressing from its subject – the personality and life of Charles Baudelaire – nevertheless takes it as the *motif* of a work of art in a way no less perfect than those of which it deals. Let me endeavour to resume the theme so that we may see the difference that more than forty years have made.

Writers and readers of to-day must necessarily look at Baudelaire with very different eyes from those of Gautier. How, why, and in what degree?

In 1857 Baudelaire published his greatest work, the volume of poems called "Les Fleurs du Mal." The book stirred literary France to its depths, and shook bourgeoisie France with horror. To many people it seemed that a veritable apostle of Satan had risen up in their midst.

In 1866 Charles Algernon Swinburne published "Poems and Ballads" and shocked literary England in precisely the same fashion, the middle classes remaining quite undisturbed and never hearing of this young man's *succès de scandale*.

The great and enduring beauty of the "Poems and Ballads," the perfection of form, incomparable music, colour-of-dreams, and of dreams alone – all these were natural products of the greatest master of metrical music since Shelley. But the *ideas* behind expression, attitude, and outlook – haunted visions of sin, swayings towards the Satanic – all these were simply drawn from Baudelaire; as Baudelaire in his fashion had distilled them from Edgar Allan Poe.

And this brings me to the point I wish to make. It is, to point out the immense influence of Baudelaire upon the literature, thought, and life of England at this very moment.

This opium-taker, the eater of hashish; the rhapsodist of emotional life divorced from any moral or unmoral impulse; the man of good birth and fine social chances who died a general paralytic; the apologist of cosmetics, the lover of panther-women and the ultimate corruption of the grave, has made a definite change in English life. All great events happen within the mind. "Waterloo," it used to be said, was "won upon the playing-fields of Eton" – just as Spion Kop was undoubtedly lost there.

An English critic of Baudelaire has said:

"The writing of a great book is the casting of a pebble into the pool of human thought; it gives rise to ever-widening circles that will reach we know not whither, and begins a chain of circumstances that may end in the destruction of kingdoms and religions and the awakening of new gods. The change wrought, directly or indirectly, by 'The Flowers of Evil' alone is almost too great to be properly understood. There is perhaps not a man in Europe to-day whose outlook on life would not have been different had 'The Flowers of Evil' never been written.

"The first thing that happens after the publication of such a book is the theft of its ideas and the imitation of its style by the lesser writers who labour for the multitude, and so its teaching goes from book to book, from the greater to the lesser, as the divine hierarchies emanate from Divinity, until ideas that were once paradoxical, or even blasphemous and unholy, have become mere newspaper commonplaces adopted by the numberless thousands who do not think for themselves, and the world's thought is changed completely, though by infinitely slow degrees. "The immediate result of Baudelaire's work was the Decadent School in French literature. Then the influence spread across the Channel, and the English Æsthetes arose to preach the gospel of imagination to the unimaginative."

These passages are illuminating. They do not enunciate a new truth, but they insist upon one which is not sufficiently recognised. Gautier has pointed out how immensely Baudelaire was influenced by Thomas de Quincey, and, especially, by Edgar Allan Poe. To continue that line of thought is my purpose.

It is impossible to mention all those French writers who are literal creations of Baudelaire, who would never have written a line had he not shown the way. Their name is Legion, and many of them do not merit the slightest attention. One great writer, however, who would never have been what he was save for Charles Baudelaire, is Verlaine.

In England, although the imitators of Baudelaire and those who have drawn inspiration from him, are far fewer in number, their influence upon English thought can hardly be over-estimated.

I do not propose to do more than outline the influence. It will be sufficient for my purpose if I take but four names; those of Algernon Charles Swinburne, Walter Pater, Oscar Wilde, and the minor poet Ernest Dowson – who produced only one small volume of verses, but who, nevertheless, belongs directly to the school of Baudelaire, and whose work is tinging the attitude towards life of the present generation in a way very little suspected by most people.

Baudelaire, when he wrote of love, invariably did so with the despair of satiety. It was always a vanished emotion that he recaptured and made beautiful in melodious verse; always the bitter taste left upon the lips of those who have kissed overmuch and overlong. The attitude is always that of the man who scourges himself, uses the rod of passion, the whip of lust, or the knout of unfulfilled desire to make some almost perfect madrigal.

It must be remembered that we are dealing with a strange and esoteric personality. I have made it my method here to be concerned with facts alone, and those who would understand the poet must be content to draw their own deductions from these facts. It is no province of mine to pass any judgment, other than the pure æsthetic. Music has come from the experiments and agonies of genius. I analyse, that is all.

The best and simplest way to make it clear how much Swinburne owed to Baudelaire is by means of parallel quotation.

Let us take, for example, Baudelaire's poem "Causerie."

"Vous êtes un beau ciel d'automne, clair et rose!
    Mais la tristesse en moi monte comme la mer,
Et laisse, en refluant, sur ma lèvre morose
    Le souvenir cuisant de son limon amer.

" – Ta main se glisse en vain sur mon sein qui se pâme;
    Ce qu'elle cherche, amie, est un lieu saccagé
Par la griffe et la dent féroce de la femme.
    Ne cherchez plus mon cœur; les bêtes l'ont mangé.

"Mon cœur est un palais flétri par la cohue;
    On s'y soûle, on s'y tue, on s'y prend aux cheveux!
– Un parfum nage autour de votre gorge nue!...

"O Beauté, dur fléau des âmes, tu le veux!
Avec tes yeux de feu, brillants comme des fêtes,
Calcine ces lambeaux qu'ont épargnés les bêtes!"

I have not included the poem in my own translations. But for
those who find that French verse still presents some difficulty, I
give an English version of "Causerie." It is fairly literal, it is more
or less melodious in English. That it quite achieves the *atmosphere*
of Baudelaire's poem I can hardly think. I have taken it from the
little volume issued by the "Walter Scott" Publishing Company,
in which, for some reason, it is called "The Eyes of Beauty."

"You are a sky of autumn, pale and rose;
But all the sea of sadness in my blood
Surges, and, ebbing, leaves my lips morose,
Salt with the memory of the bitter flood.

"In vain your hand glides my faint bosom o'er,
That which you seek, beloved, is desecrate
By woman's tooth and talon! ah; no more
Seek in me for a heart which those dogs ate.

"It is a ruin where the jackals rest,
And rend and tear and glut themselves and slay –
A perfume swims about your naked breast!

"Beauty, hard scourge of spirits, have your way!
With flame-like eyes that at bright feasts have flared
Bum up these tatters that the beasts have spared!"

Now let us come to Swinburne. If the following verses of
"Laus Veneris" in "Ballads and Poems" are not directly derived
from Baudelaire, I ask who indeed influenced the young Oxford
poet in 1886?

"Me, most forsaken of all souls that fell;
Me, satiated with things insatiable;
    Me, for whose sake the extreme hell makes mirth,
Yea, laughter kindles at the heart of hell.

"Alas thy beauty! for thy mouth's sweet sake
My soul is bitter to me, my limbs quake
    As water, as the flesh of men that weep,
As their heart's vein whose heart goes nigh to break.

"Ah God, that sleep with flower-sweet finger-tips
Would crush the fruit of death upon my lips;
    Ah God, that death would tread the grapes of sleep
And wring their juice upon me as it drips.

"There is no change of cheer for many days,
But change of chimes high up in the air, that sways
    Rung by the running fingers of the wind;
And singing sorrows heard on hidden ways."

"I dare not always touch her, lest the kiss
Leave my lips charred. Yea, Lord, a little bliss,
    Brief, bitter bliss, one hath for a great sin;
Natheless thou knowest how sweet a thing it is."

The verse of Swinburne is more musical, and has a wider range of imagery. But the passion is the same, the method is the same, and, for those who understand French as a Frenchman understands it, the "atmosphere" fails in the magic intensity that Baudelaire achieves.

This is one single instance. Those who are interested can pursue these comparisons between the two poets for themselves. They will be richly rewarded.

I have mentioned Walter Pater, that great artist in English who may be said to have succeeded Ruskin as the exponent of the most critical and refined thought of our time. When I say that he succeeded Ruskin I do not mean to imply that he has the slightest æsthetic affinity with the author of "Modern Painters." I only speak of him as having had as strong an influence upon later thought as Ruskin had upon his.

Pater was curious of everything in life and Art that offered a new sensation – that should enable men to realise themselves in the completest and most varied way. Baudelaire was certainly not

Walter Pater's master in the same degree that he was the master of Swinburne and of Wilde. Yet, none the less certainly, the Frenchman's work made expression possible to the recluse of Oxford.

Hellenic thought, with its dangerous conclusions, was restated by Pater because "Les fleurs du Mal" had paved the way.

Here again, within the compass of a brief essay it is impossible to set forth these contentions in detail. But those who have read Baudelaire, and what Gautier says about him – those who have studied contemporary thought and contemporary literature when Pater began to weave his magical prose – will confirm what is no discovery of mine, but a fact of literature. They will recognise that, in the "Conclusion" of Walter Pater's "Renaissance" the following words could hardly have been written had it not been for the daring expression of the poet whom Frenchmen admit to be second to. Hugo alone.

"The service of philosophy, of speculative culture, towards the human spirit is to rouse, to startle it to a life of constant and eager observation. Every moment some form grows perfect in hand or face; some tone on the hills or the sea is choicer than the rest; some mood of passion or insight or intellectual excitement is irresistibly real and attractive for us – for that moment only. Not the fruit of experience, but experience itself, is the end. A counted number of pulses only is given to us of a variegated, dramatic life. How may we see in them all that is to be seen in them by the finest senses? How shall we pass most swiftly from point to point, and be present always at the focus where the greatest number of vital forces unite in their purest energy?

"To burn always with this hard, gem-like flame, to maintain this ecstasy, is success in life. In a sense it might even be said that our failure is to form habits; for, after all, habit is relative to a stereotyped world, and meantime it is only the roughness of the eye that makes any two persons, things, situations, seem alike. While all melts under our feet, we may well catch at any exquisite passion, or any contribution to knowledge that seems by a lifted

horizon to set the spirit free for a moment, or any stirring of the
senses, strange dyes, strange colours, and curious odours, or work
of the artist's hands, or the face of one's friend. Not to discriminate
every moment some passionate attitude in those about us, and in
the brilliancy of their gifts some tragic dividing of forces on their
ways, is, on this short day of frost and sun, to sleep before
evening. With this sense of the splendour of our experience and of
its awful brevity, gathering all we are into one desperate effort to
see and touch, we shall hardly have time to make theories about
the things we see and touch. What we have to do is to be for ever
curiously testing new opinions and courting new impressions,
never acquiescing in a facile orthodoxy of Comte, or of Hegel, or
of our own. Philosophical theories or ideas, as points of view,
instruments of criticism, may help us to gather up what otherwise
might pass unregarded by us. 'Philosophy is the microscope of
thought' The theory or idea or system which requires of us the
sacrifice of any part of this experience, in consideration of some
interest into which we cannot enter, or some abstract theory we
have not identified with ourselves, or what is only conventional,
has no real claim upon us." What is this most perfect piece of
prose but an expansion of Baudelaire's poem "Correspondances"?

"La Nature est un temple ou de vivants piliers
Laissent parfois sortir de confuses paroles;
L'homme y passe à travers des forêts de symboles
Qui l'observent avec des regards familiers.

"Comme de longs échos qui de loin se confondent
Dans une ténébreuse et profonde unité,
Vaste comme la nuit et comme la clarté,
Les parfums, les couleurs et les sons se répondent,

"Il est des parfums frais comme des chairs d'enfants,
Doux comme les hautbois, verts comme les prairies,
 – Et d'autres, corrompus, riches et triomphants,

"Ayant l'expansion des choses infinies,
Comme l'ambre, le musc, le benjoin et l'encens,

Qui chantent les transports de l'esprit et des sens."

In the temple of night rise vast living pillars, and there those who worship murmur words that man has never yet been able to understand. The worshippers in this temple of night wander through a huge and tangled wood of symbols, while on every side they feel that inexplicable yet friendly eyes regard them.

Far-off and dim long-drawn echoes are heard. They shiver through the forest, coming together in one deep mingled sound like that of a gong. The sound reverberates and dies away.

Vast as the night and more brilliant than the day, colour, sound, sweet odours speak to the worshippers in this temple. They are all infinitely varied. There are sounds as fragrant as childhood itself. There are others as beautiful as the sound of hautbois, and the sound itself is a colour which is like green corn.

The forest is full of magic odours. The odour of amber and incense, the scent of benzoin and musk, the perfumes form themselves into one harmonic chord in which the enraptured senses and that throbbing exaltation which is of the soul, fuse into a triumphant hinting of sense and sound.

If this is not gathering the conflicting claims, bewildering experiences, the entangled interests of modern life into one receptive cistern of the brain where consciousness stands tasting all that comes, then the poem of Baudelaire means nothing, and the beautiful prose of Pater has drawn nothing from it.

"We shall see him no more"; "This is the end of the man and his work" – remarks like these only faintly indicate what was said of Oscar Wilde when he was sent to prison. When Wilde was in prison in 1896 "Salomé" was produced by Lugne Poë at the Théâtre de Louvre in Paris. England was affronted and offended. When the play of "Salomé" was produced in England for the first time it was at a private performance at the New Stage Club. The critics did their best to howl it down. It was as though a ghost, a revenant, had appeared. Meanwhile the play had been produced in Berlin, and from that moment it held the European stage. It ran for a longer consecutive period in Germany than any play by any Englishman – not excepting Shakespeare. Its popularity extended to all countries where it was not prohibited. It was performed throughout Europe, Asia, and America. It was even played in Yiddish … that was the beginning. At the present moment the works of Oscar Wilde are being sold in enormous quantities and in many editions. You can buy "Intentions" or "Dorian Gray" for one shilling. The influence that Oscar Wilde is having upon a generation of readers which has risen since he died is incalculable. Hardly an article in the daily press would be written as it is written if it were not for the posthumous prosperity of the poet whose work has risen like the Phœnix from the ashes of his personal reputation.

It was Baudelaire who provided that attitude towards life which Wilde made his gave Wilde – or rather Wilde took from Baudelaire – some of the jewels which the latter had snatched from the classic diadem of Poe.

"And if we grow tired of an antique time, and desire to realise our own age in all its weariness and sin, are there not books that can make us live more in one single hour than life can make us live in a score of shameful years? Close to your hand lies a little volume, bound in some Nile-green skin that has been powdered with gilded nenuphars and smoothed with hard ivory. It is the book that Gautier loved; it is Baudelaire's masterpiece. Open it at that sad madrigal that begins

> "'Que m'importe que tu sois sage?
> Sois belle! et sois triste!'

and you will find yourself worshipping sorrow as you have never worshipped joy. Pass on to the poem on the man who tortures himself; let its subtle music steal into your brain and colour your thoughts, and you will become for a moment what he was who wrote it; nay, not for a moment only, but for many barren, moonlit nights and sunless, sterile days will a despair that is not your own make its dwelling within you, and the misery of another gnaw your heart away. Read the whole book, suffer it to tell even one of its secrets to your soul, and your soul will grow eager to know more, and will feed upon poisonous honey, and seek to repent of strange crimes of which it is guiltless, and to make atonement for terrible pleasures that it has never known."

Thus Wilde in "Intentions." It is not an acknowledgment of what he himself owed to Baudelaire, but it is a perfectly phrased, if veiled, recognition of his debt.

The cadences of the "Madrigal Triste" are heard over and over again in the poems of Oscar Wilde. We find them in "True Knowledge," in the "New Remorse," and in "Désespoir."

In the stanzas of the "Ballad of Reading Gaol" there is much that could never have been written had it not been that Wilde was saturated with the sombre melodies of such poems as "Le Vin de l'Assassin," and "Le Vin des Chiffonniers." It was Baudelaire who suggested a literary form in which such things as were said in "Reading Gaol" could be said.

Wilde, in his earlier days, when he was writing that extraordinary poem "The Sphinx," always used to express himself as a great admirer of "Une Charogne." Mr. Sherard, Wilde's biographer, says that in his opinion the poet's admiration for that frightful and distorted work of genius was merely assumed. But Mr. Sherard tells us also that the "Flowers of Evil" exercised a great influence over Wilde's mind during the earlier period of his artistic life. And in the "Sphinx" it is most marked. Allowing for the difference of metre and the divergence of language, the two verses from Baudelaire's poem "Le Chat," which I am about to quote, are identical in thought and feeling with the opening stanzas of "The Sphinx." It is impossible not to believe – not to feel certain indeed – that when Wilde wrote –

"In a dim corner of my room for longer than my fancy thinks
A beautiful and silent Sphinx has watched me through the shifting gloom,"

he had not, consciously or unconsciously, in mind –

"Viens, mon beau chat, sur mon cœur amoureux;
Retiens les griffes de ta patte,
Et laisse-moi plonger dans tes beaux yeux,
Mêlés de métal et d'agate."

Or –

"Upon the mat she lies and leers, and on the tawny throat of her
Flutters the soft and silky fur, or ripples to her pointed ears."

and –

"Et, des pieds jusque à la tête,
Un air subtil, un dangereux parfum,
Nagent autour de son corps brun."

This should be sufficient proof in itself, but there is evidence which is absolutely conclusive. In all the criticism of Wilde's work, I do not think that any one has taken the trouble to trace these origins.

I am as certain as I am certain of anything that Wilde's poem "The Sphinx" was primarily inspired by the poem of Baudelaire in that section of "Les Fleurs du Mal" entitled "Spleen et Idéal," called "Les Chats." I have already pointed out how certain images were taken from another poem of Baudelaire, but now we are coming to the original fountain.

In the few translations I offer of Baudelaire's poems I have chosen representative verses which seem to me to express Baudelaire at his best. The poem "Les Chats" has been translated by Mr. Cyril Scott in a little volume of selections published by Mr. Elkin Mathews. Here is "Les Chats" of Baudelaire:

"Les amoureux fervents et les savants austères
Aiment également, dans leur mûre saison,
Les chats puissants et doux, orgueil de la maison,

Qui comme eux sont frileux et comme eux sédentaires.

"Amis de la science et de la volupté,
Ils cherchent le silence et l'horreur des ténèbres;
L'Érèbe les eût pris pour ses coursiers funèbres,
S'ils pouvaient au servage incliner leur fierté.

"Ils prennent en songeant les nobles attitudes
Des grands sphinx allongés au fond des solitudes,
Qui semblent s'endormir dans un rêve sans fin;

"Leurs reins féconds sont pleins d'étincelles magiques,
Et des parcelles d'or, ainsi qu'un sable fin,
Étoilent vaguement leurs prunelles mystiques."

And here is Mr. Scott's rendering:

"All ardent lovers and all sages prize,
As ripening years incline upon their brows –
The mild and mighty cats – pride of the house –
That likeunto them are indolent, stern, and wise.

"The friends of Learning and of Ecstasy,
They search for silence and the horrors of gloom;
The devil had used them for his steeds of Doom,
Could he alone have bent their pride to slavery.

"When musing, they display those outlines chaste,
Of the great sphinxes – stretched o'er the sandy waste,
That seem to slumber deep in a dream without end:

"From out their loins a fountainous furnace flies,
And grains of sparkling gold, as fine as sand,
Bestar the mystic pupils of their eyes."

I don't in the least like this translation, but the reader has only to turn to the poems of Oscar Wilde in the collected edition, issued by Messrs. Methuen – and he will find an æsthetic perspective of which the words of Baudelaire form the foreground.

Let him open the page where the reverberating words of the Sphinx begin, and it will be enough.

I shall only write a very few words about the last name on my list – that of Ernest Dowson.

This true poet, king of the minor poets as he has been called, was influenced by Baudelaire through Verlaine. As all students of modern poetry know, Ernest Dowson died a few years ago and left very little to the world – though what he left was almost perfect within its scope and purpose. I knew Dowson well, and he has often told me the debt he owed to Baudelaire. One can see it in such poems as "Cynara," which Mr. Arthur Symons says (and I thoroughly agree with him) is one of the imperishable lyrics of our literature.

And surely these two verses of "Impenitentia Ultima " –

"Before my light goes out for ever, if God should give me a choice of graces,
I would not reck of length of days, nor crave for things to be;
But cry: 'One day of the great lost days, one face of all the faces,
Grant me to see and touch once more and nothing more to see.

"'For, Lord, I was free of all Thy flowers, but I chose the world's sad roses,
And that is why my feet are torn and mine eyes are blind with sweat,
But at Thy terrible judgment-seat, when this my tired life closes,
I am ready to reap whereof I sowed, and pay my righteous debt'"

– have all the weary hunger, satiety, and unconquerable desire that over and over again glow out in such sad beauty upon the petals of the "Fleurs du Mal."

Readers who have followed me so far will observe that I have attempted hardly any criticism of Baudelaire's work. I have translated Gautier – that was the task that I set out to do. In this essay I have only endeavoured to show how Baudelaire has influenced modern English poets, who, in their turn, have made a lasting impression upon contemporary thought. I have definitely restricted the scope of my endeavour.

But I have still something to say, something concerned with the few translations I have made of Baudelaire's poems and some of the "Petits Poëmes en prose."

The prose of a French author – such is my belief – can be translated into a fair equivalent. It is a sort of commonplace for people to say that you cannot translate a foreign author into English. I feel sure that this is untrue. One cannot, of course, translate a perfect piece of French or German prose into English which has *quite* the same subtle charm of the original. Nevertheless, translation from foreign prose can be literal and delightful – but only when it is translated by a writer of *English* prose.

The reason that so many people believe, and say with some measure of justice, that French or German prose cannot be adequately translated is because they do not understand the commercial conditions which govern such work.

It is very rarely indeed that a master of English prose can find time to translate from the foreign. He is occupied entirely with his own creations. Translation, to him, would be a labour of love; the financial reward would be infinitesimal. This being so, the English public must depend upon inferior translations made by people who understand French, but are often incapable of literary appreciation, of reproducing the "atmosphere" of the authors they translate.

If Oscar Wilde had translated the French verse of Baudelaire into English verse, for example, then Baudelaire would by now be a household word. If any well-known stylist and novelist of to-day would spend a year over translating Flaubert's "Salammbô" then that masterpiece would rank with "Esmond" or "The Cloister and the Hearth" in the minds of Englishmen.

But this is too much to expect. Great creative artists are busily engaged in doing their own work, and French classics must remain more or less hidden from those lovers of literature who are not intimately conversant with the language.

We are a commercial race. Successful writers do not care to explain writers of other countries to their own countrymen. English men of letters have a deep love for English letters, but very few of them carry their amourettes over the Channel. Yet if any one doubts my contention that foreign work can be translated almost flawlessly let me remind him of John Addington Symonds' "Life of Benvenuto Cellini"; the Count Stenbock's rendering of Balzac's "Shorter Stories"; Rossetti's "La Vita Nuova" of Dante, or the translations of Maeterlinck by Mr. Teixeira de Mattos.

Charles Baudelaire, when once he had found work that appealed to him enormously, proceeded to translate it into his own language. His renderings of Poe have not only introduced Poe to the public of France, but have even improved upon the work of the American.

And Baudelaire says of his master:

"Ce n'est pas, par ces miracles matériels, qui pourtant ont fait sa renommée, qu'il lui sera donné de conquérir l'admiration des gens qui pensent, c'est par son amour du beau, par sa connaissance des conditions harmoniques de la beauté, par sa poésie profonde et plaintive, ouvragée néanmoins, transparente et correcte comme un bijou de cristal, – par son admirable style, pur et bizarre, – serré comme les mailles d'une armure, – complaisant et minutieux, – et dont la plus légère intention sert à pousser doucement le lecteur vers un but voulu, – et enfin surtout par ce génie tout spécial, par ce tempérament unique qui lui a permis de peindre et d'expliquer, d'une manière impeccable, saisissante, terrible, l'*exception dans l'ordre moral*. – Diderot, pour prendre un example entre cent, est un auteur sanguin; Poe est l'écrivain des nerfs, et même de quelque chose de plus – et le meilleur que je connaisse."

This, of course, is only a paragraph taken from a considerable essay. But with what insight and *esprit* is it not said! There is all the breadth and generality which comes from a culture, minute, severe, constantly renewed, rectifying and concentrating his impressions in a few pregnant words.

It is as well, also, that Baudelaire's marvellous *flair* for translation should be illustrated in this book. I have had some difficulty in making choice of an example, in gathering a flower from a garden so rich in blooms. I think, however, that the following parallel excerpts from "Ligeia" exhibit Poe in his most characteristic style and Baudelaire at his best in translation. (For purposes of comparison the English and the French are printed in parallel columns.)

"There is one topic, however, on which my memory fails me not. It is the *person* of Ligeia. In stature she was tall, somewhat slender, and, in her latter days, even emaciated. I would in vain attempt to portray the majesty, the quiet ease of her demeanour, or the incomprehensible lightness and elasticity of her footfall. She came and departed as a shadow. I was never made aware of her entrance into my closed study, save by the dear music of her low sweet voice, as she placed her marble hand upon my shoulder. In beauty of face no maiden ever equalled her. It was the radiance of an opium dream, an airy and spirit-lifting vision more wildly divine than the phantasies which hovered about the slumbering souls of the daughters of Delos. Yet her features were not of that regular mould which we have been falsely taught to worship in the classical labours of the heathen.

"Il est néanmoins un sujet très cher sur lequel ma mémoire n'est pas en défaut. C'est la *personne* de Ligeia. Elle était d'une grande taille, un peu mince, et même, dans les derniers jours, très amaigrie. J'essayerais en vain de dépeindre la majesté, l'aisance tranquille de sa démarche, et l'incompréhensible légèreté, l'élasticité de son pas. Elle venait et s'en allait comme une ombre. Je ne m'apercevais jamais de son entrée dans mon cabinet de travail que par la chère musique de sa voix douce et profonde, quand elle posait sa main de marbre sur mon épaule. Quant à la beauté de la figure, aucune femme ne l'a jamais égalée. C'était l'éclat d'un rêve d'opium – une vision aérienne et ravissante, plus étrangement céleste que les rêveries qui voltigent dans les âmes assoupies des filles de Délos. Cependant ses traits n'étaient pas jetés dans ce moule régulier qu'on nous a faussement enseigné à révérer dans les ouvrages classiques du paganisme.

'There is no exquisite beauty,' says Bacon, Lord Verulam, speaking truly of all forms and *genera* of beauty, 'without some *strangeness* in the proportion.' Yet, although I saw that the features of Ligeia were not of a classic regularity, although I perceived that her loveliness was indeed 'exquisite,' and felt that there was much of 'strangeness' pervading it, I have tried in vain to detect the irregularity and to trace home my own perception of the 'strange.' I examined the contour of the lofty and pale forehead – it was faultless; how cold indeed that word when applied to a majesty so divine! the skin rivalling the purest ivory, the commanding extent and repose, the gentle prominence of the regions above the temples; and then the raven-black, the glossy, the luxuriant and naturally curling tresses, setting forth the full force of the Homeric epithet, 'hyacinthine'! I looked at the delicate outlines of the nose, and nowhere but in the graceful medallions of the Hebrews had I beheld a similar perfection. There were the same luxurious smoothness of surface, the same scarcely perceptible tendency to the aquiline, the same harmoniously curved nostrils speaking the free spirit. I regarded the sweet mouth.

'Il n'y a pas de beauté exquise,' dit lord Verulam, parlant avec justesse de toutes les formes et de tous les genres de beauté, 'sans une certaine *étrangeté*, dans les proportions.' Toutefois, bien que je visse que les traits de Ligeia n'étaient pas d'une régularité classique – quoique je sentisse que sa beauté était véritablement 'exquise,' et fortement pénétrée de cette 'étrangeté,' je me suis efforcé en vain de découvrir cette irrégularité et de poursuivre jusqu'en son gîte ma perception de 'l'étrange.' J'examinais le contour de front haut et pâle – un front irréprochable – combien ce mot est froid appliqué à une majesté aussi divine! – la peau rivalisant avec le plus pur ivoire, la largeur imposante, le calme, la gracieuse proéminence des régions au-dessus des tempes et puis cette chevelure d'un noir de corbeau, lustrée, luxuriante, naturellement bouclée, et démontrant toute la force de l'expression homérique: 'chevelure d'hyacinthe.' Je considérais les lignes délicates du nez – et nulle autre part que dans les gracieux médaillons hébraïques je n'avais contemplé une semblable perfection. C'était ce même jet, cette même surface unie et superbe, cette même tendance presque imperceptible à l'aquilin, ces mêmes narines harmonieusement arrondies et révélant un esprit libre. Je regardais la charmante bouche.

Here was indeed the triumph of all things heavenly, the magnificent turn of the short upper lip, the soft, voluptuous slumber of the under, the dimples which sported, and the colour which spoke, the teeth glancing back, with a brilliancy almost startling, every ray of the holy light which fell upon them in her serene and placid, yet most exultingly radiant of all smiles. I scrutinised the formation of the chin – and here, too, I found the gentleness of breadth, the softness and the majesty, the fulness and the spirituality of the Greek – the contour which the god Apollo revealed but in a dream to Cleomenes, the son of the Athenian. And then I peered into the large eyes of Ligeia."

C'était là qu'était le triomphe de toutes les choses célestes: la tour glorieux de la lèvre supérieure, un peu courte, l'air doucement, voluptueusement reposé de l'inférieure, – les fossettes qui se jouaient et la couleur qui parlait, – les dents réfléchissant comme une espèce d'éclair chaque rayon de la lumière bénie qui tombait sur elles dans ses sourires sereins et placides, mais toujours radieux et triomphants. J'analysais la forme du menton, et là aussi je trouvais le grâce dans la largeur, la douceur et la majesté, la plénitude et la spiritualité grecques – ce contour que le dieu Apollon ne révéla qu'en rêve à Cléomène, fils de Cléomène d'Athènes. Et puis je regardais dans les grands yeux de Ligeia."

I have said, and I thoroughly believe, that it is possible for a great writer to translate the prose of another country into fine and almost literal prose of his own.

It is, however, when we come to verse that we find the literal translation inadequate. A verse translation, by the very necessity of the limits within which the artist works – that of metre and cadence – must necessarily have a large amount of freedom. The translator has first to study the poem with a care that directs itself to the dissecting, analysing and saturating himself with what the poet *means to convey*, rather than the actual words in which he conveys it. One does not translate *ventre à terre* as "belly to the earth" but as "at full gallop." The translator must have a kind of loving clairvoyance, an apprehension of inner beauty, if he is to explain another mind in the medium of poetry.

It seems unkind to instance what I mean by quoting a translation of some lines of Baudelaire which, while literally accurate, fail to give the English reader the least hinting of an atmosphere profoundly wonderful in the original.

I need not mention names, however, but will contrast the following lines –

"A languorous island, where Nature abounds
With exotic trees and luscious fruit;
And with men whose bodies are slim and astute,
And with women whose frankness delights and astounds" –

with Baudelaire's own corresponding verse from that lovely poem "Parfum exotique."

"Une île paresseuse où la nature donne
Des arbres singuliers et des fruits savoureux;
Des hommes dont le corps est mince et vigoureux,
Et des femmes dont l'œil par sa franchise étonne."

Voltaire once said of Dante that his reputation would go on

▲ 188

growing because he was so little read. That was a satire, not upon Dante, but upon humanity.

Baudelaire has a great reputation, but is still comparatively little known to English readers.

It is my hope that this translation of Gautier, and the small attempts at rendering Baudelaire, may serve as *hors d'œuvre* to a magic feast which awaits any one who cares to wander through the gates of the garden where flowers of unexampled beauty blow … and not only Flowers of Evil.

G. T.

APPENDIX

Letter from M. Sainte-Beuve
1857.

MY DEAR FRIEND,

I have received your beautiful volume, and first I have to thank you for the kind words with which it was accompanied; for a long time you have accustomed me to your good and loyal sentiments towards me. I knew some of your verses from having read them in other selections; collected together, they have quite a different effect. To say to you that this general effect is sad would not astonish you; it is what you wanted. To tell you that you have not hesitated in gathering your flowers together for any sort of image and colour, terrible and distressing though it might be, you know it better than I do; again, it is what you have wished. You are a true poet of the school of "art," and if we could talk to each other on the subject of this book, there would be much to say. You, also, are of those who look for poetry everywhere; and because, before you, others have sought it in all the easily accessible places, because you have been left little room, because the earthly and the celestial fields were rather too heavily harvested, and that for thirty years and more lyrics of all kinds have been written, because you have come so late and the last, you have said to yourself, I imagine: "Ah well, I shall still find poetry, and I shall find it where no one else has thought of gathering and extracting it," and you have taken Hell, you have made yourself devil. You wanted to wrest their secrets from the demons of the night. In doing this with subtilty, with refinement, with a careful talent, and an almost meticulous surrender of expression, in stringing the detail, in playing upon what is horrible, you seem to have been amusing yourself. You have suffered, however, you have tormented yourself to display your wearinesses, your nightmares, your moral tortures; you must have suffered much, my dear fellow. This particular sadness that shows itself in your pages, and in which I recognise the last symptom of a sick generation of whom the seniors are well known to us, is also that which you will have experienced.

You say somewhere, in marking the spiritual awakening which comes after ill-spent nights, that, when "the white and rosy dawn," appearing suddenly, comes in company with "the tormenting Ideal," at that moment, by a sort of avenging expiation –

"Dans la brute assoupie un ange se réveille!"

It is this angel that I invoke in you and that must be cultivated. If only you had let it intervene a little oftener in two or three separate places, that would have been sufficient to have disentangled your thought, so that all these dreams of evil, all these obscure forms, and all these outlandish interweavings wherein your imagination has wearied itself would have appeared in their true guise – that is to say half scattered, ready and waiting to flee before the light. Your book, then, would have yielded, like a "Temptation of St. Antony," at the moment when dawn draws near and one feels that it is about to break.

It is thus that I picture and that I understand it. One must quote oneself as an example as little as possible. But we also, thirty years ago, have sought poetry where we could. Many fields were already reaped, and the most beautiful laurels cut. I remember in what melancholy state of mind and soul I wrote "Joseph Delorme," and I am still astonished when I happen (which is rarely) to reopen this little volume, at what I have dared to say, to express in it. But, in obedience to the impulse and natural progress of my sentiments, I wrote a selection the following year, still very imperfect, but animated by a gentler, purer inspiration, "Les Consolations," and, thanks to this simple development towards good, I have been almost pardoned. Let me give you some advice which would surprise those who do not know you. You mistrust passion too much; with you it is a theory. You accord too much to the mind, to combination. Let yourself alone, do not be afraid to feel too much like others. Never fear to be common; you will always have enough in your delicacy of expression to make you distinguished.

I do not wish any longer to appear more prudish in your eyes than I am. I like more than one part of your volume – those "Tristesses de la Lune," for example, a delightful sonnet that seems like some English poet contemporary with Shakespeare's youth. It is not up to these stanzas, "A celle qui est trop gaie," which seem to me exquisitely done. Why is this piece not in Latin, or rather in Greek, and included in the section of the "Erotica" of the "Anthology"? The savant, Brunck, would have gathered it into the "Analecta veterum poetarum"; President Bouhier and La Monnoye – that is to say, men of authority and sober habits – *castissimæ vitæ morumque integerrimorum*, would have expounded it without shame and we should put on it the sign of the lovers. *Tange Chlœn semel arrogantem….*

But, once again, it is not a question of that nor of compliments. I would rather grumble, and, if I were walking with you by the side of the sea, along a cliff, without pretending to play the mentor, I should try to trip you up, my dear friend, and throw you roughly into the water, so that you, who can swim, would go straightway under the sun in full course.

Yours always,
SAINTE-BEUVE.

Beauties, Beasts, and Enchantment

CLASSIC FRENCH FAIRY TALES

Translated and with an Introduction
by Jack Zipes

A collection of 36 classic French fairy tales translated by renowned writer Jack Zipes.
Cinderella, Beauty and the Beast, Sleeping Beauty and *Little Red Riding Hood* are among the
classic fairy tales in this amazing book.
Includes illustrations from fairy tale collections.
Jack Zipes has written and published widely on fairy tales.

'Terrific... a succulent array of 17th and 18th century 'salon' fairy tales'
- *The New York Times Book Review*

'These tales are adventurous, thrilling in a way fairy tales are meant to be... The translation
from the French is modern, happily free of archaic and hyperbolic language... a fine and
sophisticated collection' - *New York Tribune*

'Enjoyable to read... a unique collection of French regional folklore' - *Library Journal*

'Charming stories accompanied by attractive pen-and-ink drawings' - *Chattanooga Times*

Introduction and illustrations   612pp.   ISBN 9781861712510 Pbk   ISBN 9781861713193 Hbk

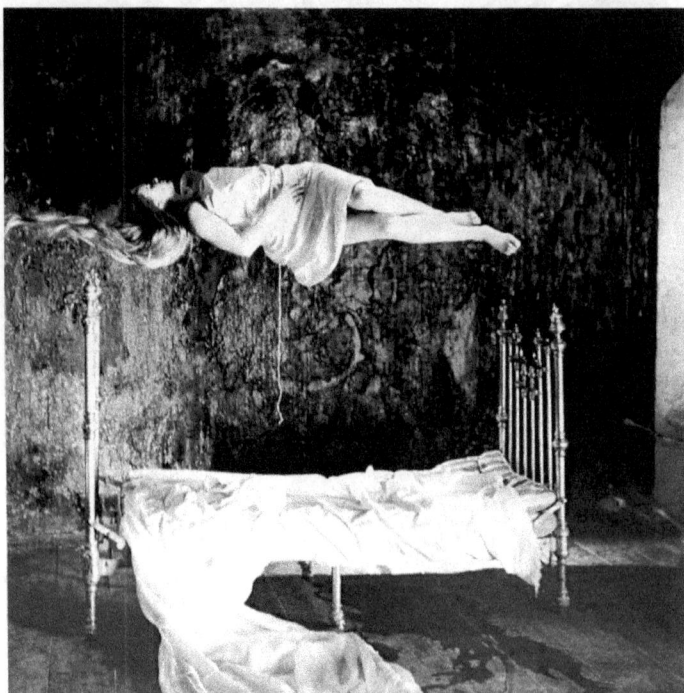

Arseny Tarkovsky

Life, Life

Selected Poems

Arseny Tarkovsky is the neglected Russian poet, father of the acclaimed film director Andrei Tarkovsky. This new book gathers together many of Tarkovsky's most lyrical and heartfelt poems, in Virginia Rounding's new, clear translations. Many of Tarkovsky's poems appeared in his son's films, such as *Mirror, Stalker, Nostalghia* and *The Sacrifice*. There is an introduction by Rounding, and a bibliography of both Arseny and Andrei Tarkovsky.

Illustrated. Bibliography and notes.
ISBN 9781861711144 Pbk   ISBN 9781861712660 Hbk

CRESCENT MOON PUBLISHING

web: www.crmoon.com e-mail: cresmopub@yahoo.co.uk

ARTS, PAINTING, SCULPTURE

The Art of Andy Goldsworthy
Andy Goldsworthy: Touching Nature
Andy Goldsworthy in Close-Up
Andy Goldsworthy: Pocket Guide
Andy Goldsworthy In America
Land Art: A Complete Guide
The Art of Richard Long
Richard Long: Pocket Guide
Land Art In the UK
Land Art in Close-Up
Land Art In the U.S.A.
Land Art: Pocket Guide
Installation Art in Close-Up
Minimal Art and Artists In the 1960s and After
Colourfield Painting
Land Art DVD, TV documentary
Andy Goldsworthy DVD, TV documentary
The Erotic Object: Sexuality in Sculpture From Prehistory to the Present Day
Sex in Art: Pornography and Pleasure in Painting and Sculpture
Postwar Art
Sacred Gardens: The Garden in Myth, Religion and Art
Glorification: Religious Abstraction in Renaissance and 20th Century Art
Early Netherlandish Painting
Leonardo da Vinci
Piero della Francesca
Giovanni Bellini
Fra Angelico: Art and Religion in the Renaissance
Mark Rothko: The Art of Transcendence
Frank Stella: American Abstract Artist
Jasper Johns
Brice Marden
Alison Wilding: The Embrace of Sculpture
Vincent van Gogh: Visionary Landscapes
Eric Gill: Nuptials of God
Constantin Brancusi: Sculpting the Essence of Things
Max Beckmann
Caravaggio
Gustave Moreau
Egon Schiele: Sex and Death In Purple Stockings
Delizioso Fotografico Fervore: Works In Process 1
Sacro Cuore: Works In Process 2
The Light Eternal: J.M.W. Turner
The Madonna Glorified: Karen Arthurs

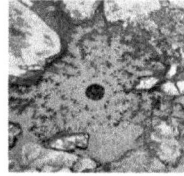

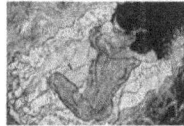

LITERATURE

J.R.R. Tolkien: The Books, The Films, The Whole Cultural Phenomenon
J.R.R. Tolkien: Pocket Guide
Tolkien's Heroic Quest
The *Earthsea* Books of Ursula Le Guin
Beauties, Beasts and Enchantment: Classic French Fairy Tales
German Popular Stories by the Brothers Grimm
Philip Pullman and *His Dark Materials*
Sexing Hardy: Thomas Hardy and Feminism
Thomas Hardy's *Tess of the d'Urbervilles*
Thomas Hardy's *Jude the Obscure*
Thomas Hardy: The Tragic Novels
Love and Tragedy: Thomas Hardy
The Poetry of Landscape in Hardy
Wessex Revisited: Thomas Hardy and John Cowper Powys
Wolfgang Iser: Essays and Interviews
Petrarch, Dante and the Troubadours
Maurice Sendak and the Art of Children's Book Illustration
Andrea Dworkin
Cixous, Irigaray, Kristeva: The *Jouissance* of French Feminism
Julia Kristeva: Art, Love, Melancholy, Philosophy, Semiotics and Psychoanalysis
Hélène Cixous I Love You: The *Jouissance* of Writing
Luce Irigaray: Lips, Kissing, and the Politics of Sexual Difference
Peter Redgrove: Here Comes the Flood
Peter Redgrove: Sex-Magic-Poetry-Cornwall
Lawrence Durrell: Between Love and Death, East and West
Love, Culture & Poetry: Lawrence Durrell
Cavafy: Anatomy of a Soul
German Romantic Poetry: Goethe, Novalis, Heine, Hölderlin
Feminism and Shakespeare
Shakespeare: Love, Poetry & Magic
The Passion of D.H. Lawrence
D.H. Lawrence: Symbolic Landscapes
D.H. Lawrence: Infinite Sensual Violence
Rimbaud: Arthur Rimbaud and the Magic of Poetry
The Ecstasies of John Cowper Powys
Sensualism and Mythology: The Wessex Novels of John Cowper Powys
Amorous Life: John Cowper Powys and the Manifestation of Affectivity (H.W. Fawkner)
Postmodern Powys: New Essays on John Cowper Powys (Joe Boulter)
Rethinking Powys: Critical Essays on John Cowper Powys
Paul Bowles & Bernardo Bertolucci
Rainer Maria Rilke
Joseph Conrad: *Heart of Darkness*
In the Dim Void: Samuel Beckett
Samuel Beckett Goes into the Silence
André Gide: Fiction and Fervour
Jackie Collins and the Blockbuster Novel
Blinded By Her Light: The Love-Poetry of Robert Graves
The Passion of Colours: Travels In Mediterranean Lands
Poetic Forms

POETRY

Ursula Le Guin: Walking In Cornwall
Peter Redgrove: Here Comes The Flood
Peter Redgrove: Sex-Magic-Poetry-Cornwall
Dante: Selections From the Vita Nuova
Petrarch, Dante and the Troubadours
William Shakespeare: Sonnets
William Shakespeare: Complete Poems
Blinded By Her Light: The Love-Poetry of Robert Graves
Emily Dickinson: Selected Poems
Emily Brontë: Poems
Thomas Hardy: Selected Poems
Percy Bysshe Shelley: Poems
John Keats: Selected Poems
Joh n Keats: Poems of 1820
D.H. Lawrence: Selected Poems
Edmund Spenser: Poems
Edmund Spenser: Amoretti
John Donne: Poems
Henry Vaughan: Poems
Sir Thomas Wyatt: Poems
Robert Herrick: Selected Poems
Rilke: Space, Essence and Angels in the Poetry of Rainer Maria Rilke
Rainer Maria Rilke: Selected Poems
Friedrich Hölderlin: Selected Poems
Arseny Tarkovsky: Selected Poems
Arthur Rimbaud: Selected Poems
Arthur Rimbaud: A Season in Hell
Arthur Rimbaud and the Magic of Poetry
Novalis: Hymns To the Night
German Romantic Poetry
Paul Verlaine: Selected Poems
Elizaethan Sonnet Cycles
D.J. Enright: By-Blows
Jeremy Reed: Brigitte's Blue Heart
Jeremy Reed: Claudia Schiffer's Red Shoes
Gorgeous Little Orpheus
Radiance: New Poems
Crescent Moon Book of Nature Poetry
Crescent Moon Book of Love Poetry
Crescent Moon Book of Mystical Poetry
Crescent Moon Book of Elizabethan Love Poetry
Crescent Moon Book of Metaphysical Poetry
Crescent Moon Book of Romantic Poetry
Pagan America: New American Poetry

MEDIA, CINEMA, FEMINISM and CULTURAL STUDIES

J.R.R. Tolkien: The Books, The Films, The Whole Cultural Phenomenon
J.R.R. Tolkien: Pocket Guide
The *Lord of the Rings* Movies: Pocket Guide
The Cinema of Hayao Miyazaki
Hayao Miyazaki: *Princess Mononoke*: Pocket Movie Guide
Hayao Miyazaki: *Spirited Away*: Pocket Movie Guide
Tim Burton : Hallowe'en For Hollywood
Ken Russell
Ken Russell: *Tommy*: Pocket Movie Guide
The Ghost Dance: The Origins of Religion
The Peyote Cult
Cixous, Irigaray, Kristeva: The *Jouissance* of French Feminism
Julia Kristeva: Art, Love, Melancholy, Philosophy, Semiotics and Psychoanalysis
Luce Irigaray: Lips, Kissing, and the Politics of Sexual Difference
Hélene Cixous I Love You: The *Jouissance* of Writing
Andrea Dworkin
'Cosmo Woman': The World of Women's Magazines
Women in Pop Music
HomeGround: The Kate Bush Anthology
Discovering the Goddess (Geoffrey Ashe)
The Poetry of Cinema
The Sacred Cinema of Andrei Tarkovsky
Andrei Tarkovsky: Pocket Guide
Andrei Tarkovsky: *Mirror*: Pocket Movie Guide
Andrei Tarkovsky: *The Sacrifice*: Pocket Movie Guide
Walerian Borowczyk: Cinema of Erotic Dreams
Jean-Luc Godard: The Passion of Cinema
Jean-Luc Godard: *Hail Mary*: Pocket Movie Guide
Jean-Luc Godard: *Contempt*: Pocket Movie Guide
Jean-Luc Godard: *Pierrot le Fou*: Pocket Movie Guide
John Hughes and Eighties Cinema
Ferris Bueller's Day Off: Pocket Movie Guide
Jean-Luc Godard: Pocket Guide
The Cinema of Richard Linklater
Liv Tyler: Star In Ascendance
Blade Runner and the Films of Philip K. Dick
Paul Bowles and Bernardo Bertolucci
Media Hell: Radio, TV and the Press
An Open Letter to the BBC
Detonation Britain: Nuclear War in the UK
Feminism and Shakespeare
Wild Zones: Pornography, Art and Feminism
Sex in Art: Pornography and Pleasure in Painting and Sculpture
Sexing Hardy: Thomas Hardy and Feminism

The Light Eternal is a model monograph, an exemplary job. The subject matter of the book is beautifully organised and dead on beam. (Lawrence Durrell)
It is amazing for me to see my work treated with such passion and respect. (Andrea Dworkin)

CRESCENT MOON PUBLISHING
P.O. Box 1312, Maidstone, Kent, ME14 5XU, Great Britain. www.crmoon.com

cresmopub@yahoo.co.uk   www.crescentmoon.org.uk

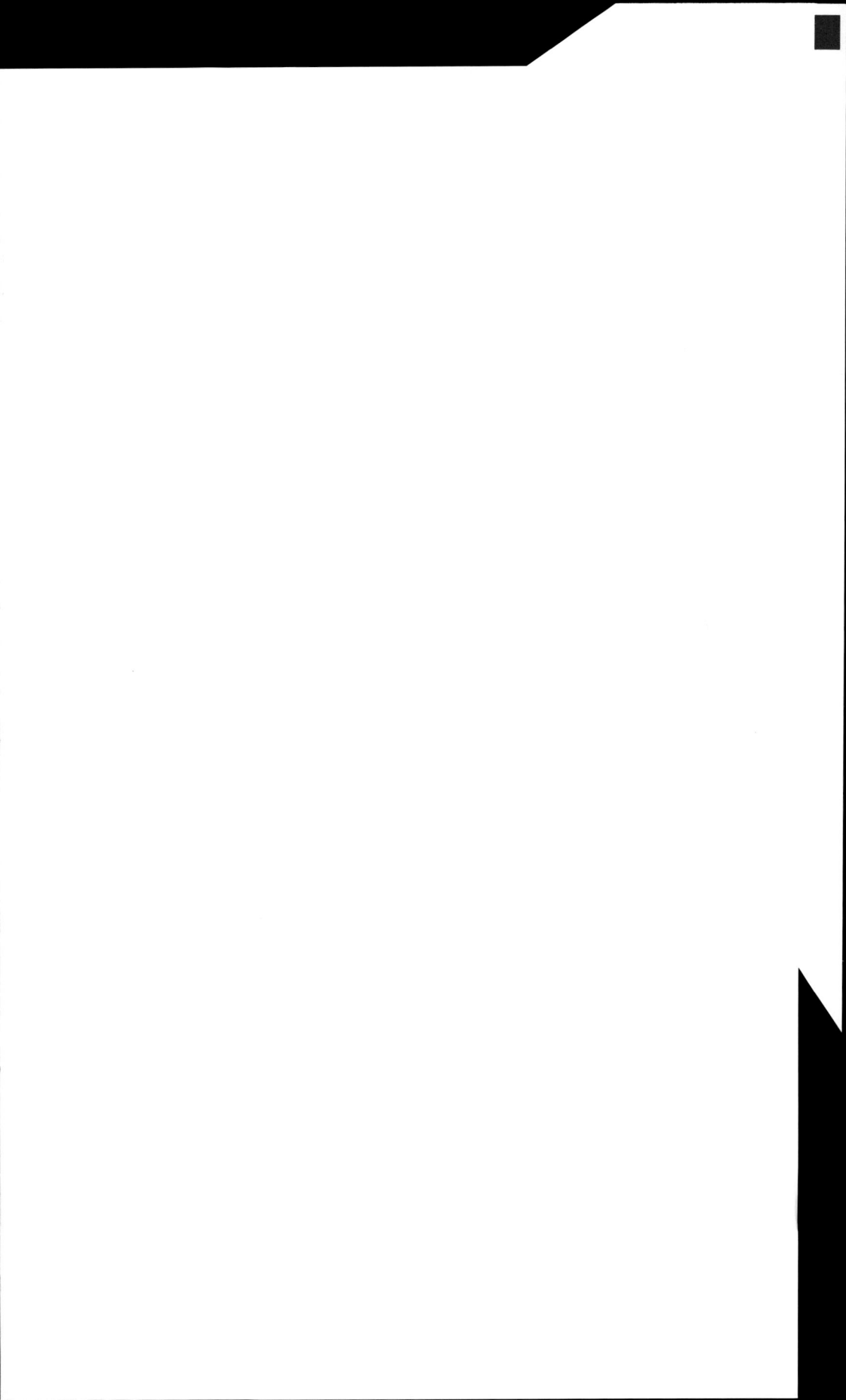

www.ingramcontent.com/pod-product-compliance
Lightning Source LLC
Chambersburg PA
CBHW062214080426
42734CB00010B/1885